# Taken Captive by Birds

**MARGUERITE POLAND**

*Illustrated by Craig Ivor*

PENGUIN BOOKS

PENGUIN BOOKS

Published by the Penguin Group
Penguin Books (South Africa) (Pty) Ltd, Block D, Rosebank Office Park, 181 Jan Smuts Avenue, Parktown North Johannesburg 2193, South Africa
Penguin Group (USA) Inc, 375 Hudson Street, New York, New York 10014, USA
Penguin Group (Canada), 90 Eglinton Avenue East, Suite 700, Toronto, Ontario, Canada M4P 2Y3 (a division of Pearson Penguin Canada Inc)
Penguin Books Ltd, 80 Strand, London WC2R 0RL, England
Penguin Ireland, 25 St Stephen's Green, Dublin 2, Ireland (a division of Penguin Books Ltd)
Penguin Group (Australia), 250 Camberwell Road, Camberwell, Victoria 3124, Australia (a division of Pearson Australia Group Pty Ltd)
Penguin Books India Pvt Ltd, 11 Community Centre, Panchsheel Park, New Delhi – 110 017, India
Penguin Group (NZ), 67 Apollo Drive, Rosedale, Auckland 0632, New Zealand (a division of Pearson New Zealand Ltd)

Penguin Books (South Africa) (Pty) Ltd, Registered Offices:
Block D, Rosebank Office Park, 181 Jan Smuts Avenue, Parktown North Johannesburg 2193, South Africa

www.penguinbooks.co.za

First published by Penguin Books (South Africa) (Pty) Ltd 2012
Reprinted 2012

Copyright text © Marguerite Poland 2012
Copyright illustrations © Craig Ivor van Vuuren 2012

All rights reserved
The moral right of the author has been asserted

ISBN 978-0-14-353044-2

Cover by Michiel Botha
Printed and bound by Imago

Except in the United States of America, this book is sold subject to the condition that it shall not, by way of trade or otherwise, be lent, resold, hired out or otherwise circulated without the publisher's prior consent in any form of binding other than that in which it is published and without a similar condition including this condition being imposed on the subsequent purchaser.

Marguerite Poland:

For my daughters Susan and Verlie
and for Martin, Ross, Greg, Jack, Eva-Wren, Alexandra Hope
and my sister Nicki

with my love

Craig Ivor van Vuuren:

With my love to my grandparents

Albie and Madeleine van Vuuren

and

Hennie and Margaret Truter

I am so blessed and thankful for who you are and what you mean to me

# CONTENTS

Acknowledgements     vii
Introduction     1

Chapter One | *Owls*     5
Chapter Two | *Poultry*     11
Chapter Three | *Dikkops*     19
Chapter Four | *Robin And Thrush*     27
Chapter Five | *Swallows*     35
Chapter Six | *Hoopoes And Drongos*     41
Chapter Seven | *Paradise Flycatcher*     49
Chapter Eight | *Spreeus*     57
Chapter Nine | *Hawks*     63
Chapter Ten | *Bee Eaters*     71
Chapter Eleven | *Crows*     81
Chapter Twelve | *Shrikes*     89
Chapter Thirteen | *Doves*     97
Chapter Fourteen | *Game Birds*     103
Chapter Fifteen | *Jiza Birds*     111
Chapter Sixteen | *Wagtails*     119
Chapter Seventeen | *Nightjars*     129
Chapter Eighteen | *Gull*     139

# ACKNOWLEDGEMENTS

**MARGUERITE POLAND**

With grateful and loving thanks to:

Craig Ivor, for whom I have the greatest admiration, for his superbly sensitive drawings without which this memoir could not have been completed, and to my daughter, Suzannah Garland, for introducing me to his work.

Martin Oosthuizen, my husband, who nudged me into showing him my essays, who edited meticulously and with humour and who patiently indulged my anxieties, and our daughters, Susie and Verlie, for their loving response.

Alison Lowry and Pam Thornley, my editors at Penguin, for the many years of warm friendship and greatly valued professional commitment and especially to Reneé Naudé and the whole production team at Penguin for their care and enthusiasm.

Alan Fogarty for revisiting the birds of The Bush for me with such knowledge and generosity, and my sister Nicki de Villiers for shared memories and laughter.

My childhood friends, Liz Bell, Lesley Mason and the Fogartys – for being there.

And for Barbara Bailey – for Believing.

## CRAIG IVOR VAN VUUREN

With my thanks to:

Marguerite Poland for giving me this valuable and life-changing experience. You paint with words. This journey with you has been the start of a new path in life that I will walk with pride.

Warwick Tarboton for your magnificent photography. Your appreciation and love of Nature's finest details – from dragonflies to birds – is inspiring. And to Geurt Bloem for the photograph of the crow.

My family for your unconditional love and support which is deeply appreciated. Thank you for believing in me – I love you.

# *Introduction*

*The artist tries to give tangible meaning*
*To those visible and spiritual presences*
*That give context to his daily life.*

(Isadore Okpewho 1979: 27)

In Zulu there is a saying, '*Ngithunjwe izinyoni*' – I have been taken captive by birds. It indicates that the work of keeping seed-eaters from the ripening crops leaves no time for anything else. But being taken captive by birds has other meanings too: to enter an awareness of another sphere; to apprehend more fully those melodious hidden places of the *jiza* bird, observed yet mythopoeic; to hear minutely the quiet rustling in the undergrowth, the popping notes of bou bous, the little gong of the tinker barbet's anvil, never seen but somewhere in the dappled shade of summer days. To know the trickle of the oriole, the hollow bubbling of the coucal.

Even if I do not know the scientific names of the birds I love, I know their mythologies, the skein that weaves them to the human world: the sorrow of birds, their cruelties and their tenderness, their triumphs and caprices, their artistry.

I have no sentiment about them in the sense of wanting ownership. I could not bear to keep a bird in a cage. The closest to ownership that I could come is to covet the reassembled skeletons in the store of the museum where I once worked: something in the engineering of those stark, fragile sculptures, their foxed, handwritten labels, a sense of the rigour – or the cunning – of the long-gone collector, the taxidermist's skill.

More than skeletons, I love birds' eggs. I remember a collection of them in an old storeroom on a farm, laid out in rows, in families, in species: from the smallest – frail as a soap bubble – to the heavy, creamy globes of ostrich eggs. I loved best the soft blue and pewter-spotted shells, the pale green and taupe, the glossy rust to brown, the ovals pared to a point, even the simple white of doves' eggs – snowy buds, waiting to unfurl.

And, of course, there are birds which are especially beloved.

They are the secretive and cryptic, companions to the traveller on the road, the good-luck birds. I much prefer the camouflaged to the bright and gaudy – quails and francolins, little brown seed-blown sparrows, larks and pipits and longclaws which haunt the tussocks of the grasslands. There are prinias and bleating bush warblers in whose brown plumage is more subtlety than in the gaudiest wings or plumed tails.

The most tender of all is the wagtail. Small, grey clockwork creature swaying on its splinter legs, it trips across the lawn, through flower beds, along the warm brick path, companionable and trusting. Then, at night, when the moon is full, there is the crying of the dikkops on the lawn. It is the comfort before sleep, akin to the distant surging of the sea, far off across the bush-covered dunes: a wave washing in, then retreating into silence. And I know – somewhere the moon is rising over the flatlands and the sea.

But the voice which beckons to the quietest spaces of the heart is the call of the fiery-necked nightjar. On summer nights, from the most secret recesses of the bush, comes the beckoning tremble of the nightjar's call. Mottled as the leaf-mould on which it rests, monogamous, courageous in its long migration south, the small wanderer comes home each year to its familiar dark.

Here, in my garden, now, is the Cape robin. Almost mouse-like in its sudden darts and scutterings from shrub to shrub, its swift alightings, its sickle-swift departures, bold enough to come within inches of my hoe. It has been there for years – or so it seems, busily and bossily defending its territory. I hear it as the green dawn washes in, its flutings clear beneath the chittering of bulbuls in the trees.

It has become my companion, my *igugu* – the precious one – associated with those I love the dearest.

Not long ago our younger daughter and her husband bought a house. The reason for their choice was a slim stained glass window on the stairwell in the centre of which perches a bold robin. Now as we descend the stairs I say to three small people, barely able to negotiate the steps:

–There is the robin.

And together, they purse up their lips and try to whistle, cocking a beady eye at the little bird that watches from its lofty height.

It is appropriate then, that my childhood home was named, in Xhosa, *Kwezintaka* – the place of birds. If, for reasons which will be explained, the name was changed to something comfortably English and predictable, it remains, in my memory, the haunt of multitudes of birds, mostly small and unremarkable, but, to me, essential to the sense of what is 'home'.

Their doings are the thread that runs through childhood, the link to people and to place. Their appearance and their presence can at once recall a name, a scent, a morning full of song and exploration, an evening sorrow, a childhood fear. A dream.

My family – our parents, Jumbie and Hopie, and our grandmother, Ninngy – came to the valley which the locals called *The Bush* in 1952 when my sister Nicky and I were very young. It was a small community strung along a coastal valley threaded by a white-lime road leading to a long stretch of unspoiled beach. The properties were large – upwards of ten acres each. Some of the landowners farmed dairy cows, most kept horses. Nearly all the children in the neighbourhood had ponies.

Men worked in town, in businesses and banks. Many were professional. Women stayed at home. Gardens bloomed, children thrived. The houses, if unpretentious, were large and staffed with 'servants'.

The children did everything together. Play-days rotated round the neighbourhood, Hopie whizzing about in her Morris Minor to collect or deliver from house to house. The grown-ups played together too: tennis and tea, dinners and picnics, drinks parties every Sunday under someone's trees or on a wide veranda – the waiting Sunday roast drying out in ovens all over the valley.

Christmas was a great communal celebration.

But there was another community as well. The farm workers and the labourers, the domestics and the itinerant woodcutters in their donkey carts, plying slowly down the side paths, their cart tracks criss-crossing the deeper bush that ran a mile-wide seam of impenetrable tangle between the southern boundaries of the properties and the rocky coast and sea.

Like bush birds, secret in the smallest clearings in the thickets, another life unfolded.

And, like the detritus of the city dumps which had been scattered on that flatland a century before and over which the ubiquitous Port Jackson aliens had spread, these discarded people eked out their existence, taking their small offerings and earnings to the Cash Store near the last cattle grid which marked the entrance to this world.

Somehow, it was the birds that saw it all: those unobtrusive harbingers whose boundaries are defined by other laws than ours but whose ancient lore remains a cipher of remembrance for me.

By these, from earliest childhood, I believe I was taken captive.

*Marguerite Poland*
*Grahamstown*
*March 2012*

# CHAPTER ONE
## *Owls*

*T*hen there was the owl.

He used to sit in the multi-trunked milkwood at the edge of the garden, in the lonely littoral zone where the cultivated beds of English flowers ended and the rough stretch of lawn with its dank green reservoir and generator shed gave way to the impenetrable, thorny barrier of bush past which it was impossible to go.

That tree was sinister. He was its denizen.

Sometimes I would see him, high up in the crown – he with his ear tufts, a sentinel silhouetted against the sky. I recall the hunched weight of him, the slow turn of his head, the last light making him a cut-out shadow bird with angry eyes. I never knew if he roosted in that tree with its multiple trunks, its brown-grey shadows and its spidery bark where stinging caterpillars clung or if it was just a favoured vantage point at dusk.

We had been warned to keep away from it: it was a haven for snakes.

But I wonder now if the mandate was really for the snakes. More likely, it was the owl and the lurking fragment of legend that still clung to the property and which linked the owl, the tree and the outbuildings on the south side of the house.

When we arrived, no one would consent to work there. Not until we changed the name of the house, *Kwezintaka*, the Place of Birds – and its association. In a valley, where workers had lived for generations, it was avoided as a place of evil omen, of tragedy.

Two or three years before we arrived, a family of farm workers had been asphyxiated in the room next to the coal cellar. Lighting a brazier at night, the windows and doors closed against the cold, they had inhaled carbon monoxide and died.

Hopie, our mother, might have asked why it had happened: if it had been intentional or if it was an accident. Nicky and I were too small to know these things – and yet, something in the cold shadow of the corner where the stable door hung at an angle at the entrance to that room, the mossy drip of a pipe bandaged with hessian and tied with wire, the dank smell of wet concrete, the gloom of the open coal shed abutting it, gave it an air of dimness and despair. We would tiptoe past, our hearts fluttering in our throats, the little shards of coal and anthracite spiteful under our bare feet.

When I was older I might lie awake at night and listen for the owl, imagining its sudden soundless flight sweeping across the house and lawn, the outbuildings and the coal shed next to which, in that unventilated room, a family had died. Forever, the smell of anthracite being shovelled into the Aga stove left a wisp of death in its scent, as fleeting as the flush of the owl's wing in flight.

There was no separating them.

The name, *Kwezintaka*, had to go.

It was replaced with something sturdily Scottish – *Penderley* – echoing our father, Jumbie's, recent origins. The walls were whitewashed, the lawns were mowed, the black-soiled sandy beds were dug over and edged with chunks of limestone, the undergrowth around a copse of milkwoods undercut, swept bare and planted with hardy shrubs.

Two families came, at last, to work. One for the house, one for the garden.

Breeze-block quarters were built for them at either end of the eleven-acre plot with steel windows and stable doors and enough draught and ventilation between the rafters and the asbestos roofs to ensure that asphyxiation would not be a concern.

Damp and asbestosis were more pressing possibilities – but those were overlooked.

For me, it was an adventure to go between two worlds, the long white house with its new English name and the little dark staff houses in their clearings, like the nests of bush birds hidden in the undergrowth.

Even the owl seemed less obtrusive then.

Only sometimes he would call and I, afraid, would make the dash down the long passage past the dark cavern of the bathroom to Hopie's bed.

Safe from the brush of his wing and the whisper of Death.

# CHAPTER TWO
# *Poultry*

*N*inngy, our grandmother, loved ducks and chickens. The ducks came first. The chickens next: a hen and a half-grown brood. The ducks had been bought to hunt snails in the flower garden, the chickens were a gift and kept in the romantic hope of eggs.

Eggs we did not get.

The genets, rats and snakes usually took their toll.

The brown hen and her chicks used to accompany Ninngy round the garden in her perambulations from bed to bed with her bucket or her trowel. Behind, strutting with a sort of vulgar propriety was the handsome cock.

Alert to all intrusion, the olive thrushes that foraged in the dewy early morning flower borders would dart off, giving way – offended – to the strange procession: grandmother, two dachshunds, sometimes the large ginger cat, the hen and chicks and the rooster herding all before him.

Following, at a little distance, James Raga, the gardener, with the large black hosepipe, dragging it looped across his shoulder. He had a thin, ascetic face and wore a handkerchief knotted at the corners on his head which he used occasionally to wipe the sweat away.

Keeping at a distance were the white ducks, the snail-eaters, who were not supposed to trample seedlings or uproot newly planted poppies. But the female – neck stretched out – cut a swathe through everything in her anxiety to get away from her amorous mate. He was a rampant duck! He flung himself on her back more than he waddled at her side. And, at last, he killed her, having pecked the feathers from her neck, leaving it raw and suppurating. One day, she simply lay down and died.

'Oh, Hopie,' Ninngy lamented, a quiver in her voice which, in hindsight, echoed all her hidden notions of the perfidy of men. 'Don't tell the children.'

–Don't tell the children.

It is a plaintive thread that weaves its way through childhood.

The ever-present undertow beneath both the simple and the numinous.

The chickens had been a gift from Mrs Duma, the teacher at the farm school for which Hopie had raised funds and then supervised the building. The Duma chickens arrived in a cardboard box which she'd carried down herself one afternoon. They were kept in the tack room until James Raga had made a sturdy *hok* with chicken wire and creosoted poles beside the water tank above the vegetable garden.

I am not sure that Hopie had the time or inclination for chickens but Ninngy and I were enchanted. The hen was pale brown and very plump. Her feathers were soft fans of biscuit edged with white and her comb flopped above her eye like a velvet pansy on a fat lady's little hat, tipped at an angle. I called her Dodie because she reminded me of Dodie who lived down the road, all big bosom and plumpness with rather thin, shapely calves. She stepped deftly despite her weight, always eager after information – pecking here, pecking there – somehow feathery with talcum powder and angora wool, shedding little trails of fluff and down from her cardigans. She had bright brown eyes and looked about her, never quite finding anything on which to focus for too long. But she made proper puddings that never came from a packet like ours did and sponge cakes with icing in the middle instead of thrifty jam.

James Raga owned the cock which joined the chickens when they were released from the *hok* in the mornings. He was a tall, spurred, black-plumed rake with strong, yellow-putteed legs. If more imperious, he was less demanding than the white drake which had disappeared soon after the demise of his mate. I am sure he ended up in the Ragas' cooking pot. Quietly removed (–Don't tell the children), his neck hastily wrung.

Nothing more was said.

Hopie, always gracious, had accepted the chickens and Mrs Duma had enjoyed a cup of tea with her and discussed the arrangements for Prize Giving and the end-of-term Christmas party. She had brought the Reverend Mr Msizi with her. He was an old clergyman who took the service in the school once a month when it doubled as a chapel. To Hopie's exasperation our father Jumbie always called him 'an old *skelm*' – no doubt because he was usually a supplicant for funds.

The Reverend Msizi knew – and even I knew then, instinctively – that there was no one else in the valley who would have helped but Hopie, no one who would have had him for tea in the living room and served it in china cups and talked to him without the least discomfort.

He was a dear old man with a wall eye and no teeth. I remember the pinkness of his gums and their mottling, the shine of his bald head, his carefully starched dog collar and his old tweed jacket. He carried a stick, walking as if he had a leg at each corner, tipping gently from side to side. He must have been nearing eighty. What tales he might have told of his provenance, his early training, the rich mission history out of which he must have come.

But no one ever asked him. And so he never said.

Jumbie – polite bluster, immensely hearty – always had urgent business with the generator while Hopie and the Reverend Msizi sat serenely in the living room and Mrs Duma stirred her tea: I can still hear the thunks of the heavy teaspoon against the rim of the green china cup while a plate of Ninngy's peanut biscuits was passed around until it was empty but for crumbs.

It must have been a lonely life for Mrs Duma in that little school tucked in the bush with no one within her own community who was as educated as she. She cultivated mealies. She grew pumpkins, she had chickens. A Bible always lay on the table in her small room, on a crocheted doily. And Mrs Duma spent her Saturdays alone.

One holiday – our terms being different – I asked if I could come to school and be part of her class. If she was astonished she did not say. And so when the housemaid's children went to school one Monday morning I accompanied them, going across the old rusty grid and walking up the lime-white road to the three-cornered stile gate in the hedge. The path was worn by passersby, a furrow of fine black sand, the roots of brush threaded across it and ready to noose unwary feet.

The schoolchildren were in the playground: a stretch of bare earth, some tussocks of Kikuyu grass and a tap. Laid out at the side of the house was an abundant vegetable garden: cabbages and mealies, beans and small tomatoes, radishes and spinach and a fine spiky pumpkin vine decked with great gold flowers. Mrs Duma's chickens ran long-legged in and out of the bush – thin, colourful, wild fowls used to dodging human interference.

We sat at desks in the school room, forty or so of us ranging from five-year-olds to big lads of fifteen. Mrs Duma was the only teacher, trying to juggle the curriculum to cover all.

The pupils waited their turn, hour on hour. The floor underfoot was made of cow dung. Something of the little feet that scuffed it gave the air a blue, furry softness, a hazy feel. On the window sills stood four plaster angels. They were a reminder that the schoolroom was also a church. The altar, doubling as a desk, stood at the head of the room. The rafters were bare, the Bible pictures on the walls were tacked to a wooden picture rail with drawing pins.

Real reverence is rare. But I recall the sense of it as I stood in the dappled light of the schoolroom. Sunbeams filtered down through the places where the rivets held the creaking roof and made limpid flowers of light all about the feet of the children, arms held up and bent across each other like a raft before the chest – an attitude of prayer quite unfamiliar to me as they recited the Lord's Prayer in Xhosa:

*UBawo wethu osezulwini . . .*

The young voices dipped and fluted gently, the rise and fall of tone and tempo. The sound recalled, years later, the soft chorus of redwinged starlings in the autumn trees – a melancholy, unobtrusive, plaintive sound.

I asked Mrs Duma if she would teach me Xhosa.

She agreed – and on Wednesday afternoons, after school, she would walk down and sit with me at the dining room table, not quite knowing where to start.

So we began with chickens.

*Inkuku:* fowl. *Umqhagi:* cock.

She made me say the click over and over, gently shaking her head at my ineptitude.

More interesting to her than my vague thrusts and rushes at the words, were the merry conversations which she had with Jane Djantjes in the kitchen afterwards or tea with Hopie in the living room.

I think for Mrs Duma it was a welcome outing – for me, a notion which I did not have the discipline to carry through. The lessons ended in disarray, rather like the venture into keeping chickens.

The cockerel did not peck his lady nor even disturb the pert angle of her crest. He was protective always, except that he was unable to keep her eggs and chickens safe. First there were six chicks. Then there were three. Only two, more wily that the rest, seemed destined to grow to maturity.

Searches for the missing chicks were fruitless. They had been spirited away.

Sure that the raider came at night, I searched the *hok* for a point of entry – the foundations dug, the nest overturned, the door ajar. But it was serene in its sturdy security.

It was finally discovered late one afternoon when the heat had sent the chickens back to the *hok* and a shrill cacophony of squawks arose. Slack, yellow, patterned kei-apple yellow, tobacco juice and sand, the thief was an enormous puff adder. It could pull itself quite easily through the holes of the wide-mouthed chicken wire.

James Raga, knowing the ways of snakes and hearing the cockerel's warning squawk, brought his snake stick – pronged, hinged and bound round with sacking, caught it deftly by the neck, clamping it in the cushioned vice. I stood behind the wall with my sister, Nicky, too afraid to approach except behind her, holding onto her shirt as she – much braver – went to look.

The puff adder was sluggish, recently fed. 'I bet there are at least three of our chickens in there,' said Nicky knowingly.

The snake was lowered into a double hessian sack and the neck secured with a twist of wire. The sack lay venomous and faintly moving, as if it had lungs. It was put in the boot of the Morris Minor and when Hopie set off for town next day, the snake went with her to the Snake Park on the hill behind the tall Edwardian Museum which smelled of formalin and was filled with stuffed animals.

Seven and sixpence a foot. That was the standard rate of pay for a live snake.

It was good enough to display in a glass case with a stunted *spekboom* plant and a little trough of water, a warm, electrically lighted rock and a regular supply of white mice for its feed.

The snake which had eaten Dodie's chickens became an exhibit. It was probably given a name.

And James Raga had an extra few shillings to add to his wages.

After that, the chicken *hok* was empty and Dodie and her cockerel joined James Raga's bush fowls and became, in time, as wild and wily as they. They lost their anthropomorphic associations and their names. They were simply chickens again.

And, briefly, for Nicky and me, rabbits were more interesting.

**CHAPTER THREE**
*Dikkops*

*D*ikkops crying on the lawn at dusk. To hear them and the ribbon of sound, *pi-pi-pi-pi-pi*, weaving through the darkness, is to be transposed to the long white-walled bungalow, the paraffin lamps lit at evening, the silhouette of trees against a sky the colour of *isipingo* berries, mauve and pewter grey.

My *umlolozelo*, my childhood lullaby.

The first time I recall a dikkop's nest was at our neighbours, the Morelands. Coming round the curve of the drive towards the old thatched-roofed farmhouse late one afternoon, I was suddenly aware of the swift flash of an eye, the deeply streaked brown body of a large ground bird standing still and erect on its yellow legs, emerging suddenly from its surroundings – a trick of light, of optics – and re-submerging just as swiftly into the camouflage of undergrowth. There – not one, but two – under the Pride of Madeira where the leaves fell thick and the mower never went.

'I saw dikkops on your lawn,' I said, pointing.

'Yes,' said Tom Moreland, coming to greet us. 'They have a nest there. They have used that spot for years. Got to watch out for the eggs. Damned dogs used to get them.'

The damned dogs were too old now to care. They were fat Scotties – rather bristly and smelly with boot-button black eyes and burrs clogged on the thick dark kilts of their underbellies. They were not fond of children.

I did not know the little ambiguities of life when I was nine. How could I?

The dikkop's tenuous existence: feigning death, lying prone, standing still almost to the point of capture; afraid of dogs, the mower, the gardener, the careless passersby, the boomslang in the Pride of Madeira, the meercat in the grass.

Just hoping to exist.


What makes a man a hero in a child's eyes?

Tom was a hero to me. It was nothing that he did or said, nothing that he presently was. He was simply a landowner on a small, inherited property, making the best of it with dairy and vegetables. But there was such an air of old-world gallantry and glamour, it was as if his Royal Flying Corps wings were still pinned to his chest, as if he was still flying the endless upturned lakes of blue above the vast plains of German East Africa in 1916 or blazing away above the battlefields of France. They say a pilot's life expectancy in the Great War was only eleven days – and he could have been no more than twenty at the time.

There was something of the camaraderie of the Mess in the way he spoke to Jumbie despite the different wars in which they'd served, a generation apart. And no, they never talked about the War or anything more particular than the state of the Bedford truck or the incompetence of the farm workers – paternalistic as District Commissioners amongst the troublesome tribesmen! And yet, in the ease of movement, the loose-limbed alertness, even as an old man with liver spots all up his wiry arms, there was a sense of treasure troves of knowledge and experience about Tom: of daring, grit; of desert storms and Channel winds; of battles and 'kills' and moments which were never ever mentioned. An aura, like a battle hymn.

Perhaps I simply imagined this for I'd once heard Jumbie say to Hopie, 'Got more gongs than a general and damned good show too!'

And yet there was nothing military or distant about Tom. I can remember his laugh, the way he pulled his shoulders up and shook in silent, generous mirth, his kindliness to children, his deference to Nora, his wife, his courtliness to Hopie.

Tea was served in summer on the veranda. It was deep as a three-sided room with low windows under the thatch, open on one side to the garden with its milkwoods and knobthorns and *boerboons* all neatly trimmed and grassed beneath.

The veranda flags were polished red and the Scottie dogs' nails clicked briskly on them as they walked. The square table was set in a bow-windowed recess with an embroidered cloth and chintz window seats. Then Daniel, the cook, would arrive in his white suit and dark blue apron, his whitewashed tackies and his black impassive face.

He was from East Africa. He had come south with the family almost forty years before. They declared he was 'part of the family'.

Whatever that may mean to a man in an apron and tackies whose task it is to heave a tea trolley, twice a day, over the lip of the stairs and wheel it, tinkling, to the table.

After the blue and white Italian Spode teacups and plates had been laid out, he reappeared with the silver. Teapot, milk jug, hot water beaker fluted with elegant spouts and ivory knobs and handles. The sugar basin was embossed with entwined initials and a date: a wedding gift to Tom and Nora in 1919, the Great War over.

Daniel always made the scones.

There was no one who made scones like 'Daniel Moreland'. It was Nora's recipe of course, but Daniel made the scones his own way and they flaked off in the thinnest layers beneath the knobbly knuckles of their crowns to steam gently, waiting for the butter and the jam and cream.

The Moreland cream was legendary. It was so thick it could not be poured, so rich that a guest, coming once for Christmas, ate a bowl of it with brown sugar as a treat and stayed in bed for three days with a bilious attack.

'Silly fool!' Jumbie had said.

'If he hadn't eaten the cream you'd have had to entertain him!' Hopie had retorted tartly.

That had cheered Jumbie up no end.

Whenever we visited the Morelands I always asked, very tentatively, picking at the edge of the table until a frown from Hopie stopped me and made me curl sweaty fingers into my lap, if I could see Nora's old-fashioned doll. She knew I would ask and she had told Daniel to open the loft room with his bunch of keys.

'You know where to go,' she said, dabbing at her mouth with her little square of starched white napkin. 'I can't manage the stairs any more.'

I got down, slipping quietly past the twitching Scotties in case one – startled – leapt up with a growl.

The living room had a huge fireplace with a high dark mantel on which was a clock and a collection of photographs in silver frames, a pipe stand with a range of dark-bowled pipes, a pair of china dogs. There were etchings and landscapes, deep chintz sofas and a long refectory table with Windsor chairs. I went through the stable door to the passage which led to the whitewashed kitchen, past the dim pantry and the hat stand on which there still hung an old pith helmet – that most colonial of trappings – part of the uniform of the men who had served in East Africa long ago.

Daniel moved like a shadow in the doorway and smiled, indicating the way. He had a long face and long teeth and his hair, threaded with grey, was brushed back and up, the faintest parting dividing its thick dignified sponginess.

He watched me as I climbed the steps, vigilant that I should not fall between the slats for it was an outside staircase leading to the loft. I was level with the tops of the milkwoods when I reached the little landing, the brightness of their waxy leaves clustered at my feet. The door to the loft was ajar. I pushed it open: such a soft, cobwebby gloom. It rustled with rain spiders.

The doll in its carriage had been brought to the front of the lumber. It lay very quietly among the foxed, embroidered sheets, a face of wax, tinted faintly at the cheeks, vacant eyes staring up. Nora had once told me that the hair was real. After that I did not dare to touch it for I believed that real hair belonged to someone dead. It was a dull auburn and seemed sticky. The little hands, plump with dimples at each knuckle, were folded at its side. Button boots, trimmed lawn petticoat, muslin frock. It was, I suppose, my idea of quintessential England – of which I had no idea beyond the pink parts on the world map at school, the hankies in slim boxes sent to Ninngy by a sister and Callard and Bowser's Butterscotch which accompanied the gift each year. Nicky and I were always given one piece each – *By Appointment to her Majesty the Queen* – neat in its lined silver wrapper, to be licked and examined, never crunched.

I always spoke to the doll in the pram, believing all inanimate things alive to hear. But she only stared ahead with her faint cleft chin and her small pink mouth. I wondered if she would like to go outside and feel the sun and look out from the platform at the top of the stairs, right over the bush towards the sea. Perhaps, from there, we would be able to see across the lawn to where the dikkops nested under the Pride of Madeira.

I lifted her gingerly, afraid that I may not be allowed to hold her. The arms flopped back despite the stiff, smooth, dimpled roundness. I peeped under the muslin dress to see the whole of her. She had bloomers and petticoats with covered buttons all the way up the front.

But her body was cloth.

It was a shock.

If she didn't have a body, she couldn't have a heart. If she did not have a heart, she was not alive. If she was not alive – she could not hear me speak.

She wasn't real after all.

I put her back in the pram and went away.

As I tiptoed towards the door, alert for flatties on the rafters above my head, I saw the black-framed stacks of photos leaning up against each other at the angle where the thatch met the floor.

Stooping to run a finger over the glass of one, making a trail through its rime of dust, I found a photograph of Tom as a young man. Tall, rangy in his flying uniform, his goggles dangled from his hand. Behind him was his fragile plane, palm trees in the distance. Incongruously, at his side, in a uniform as well – if a workman's overall – but military, smart, and bandoliered, was Daniel, to attention, grinning. The same long teeth, the same parting in the hair.

A pilot and his batman; comrades-in-arms.

Daniel was standing in the doorway to his room when I went down, very still, the shadow deep behind him, his uniform starkly white, his dark face and head so shadowed I imagined rather than saw them.

I did not know the word detachment then. But I sensed its meaning. There he was – a relic, quite detached – from someone else's past.

And, like the dikkops – in the face of odds too great – just hoping to exist.

CHAPTER FOUR

*Robin and Thrush*

*T*here is something very bold and independent about a Cape robin. One used to dart about in the flower beds at Penderley. Through all the years I believed it was the same bird: companionable, constant and cheerful. But I never found its nest – try as I might to discover it.

It evaded me, singing blithely from another bush, gently warning me away.

The other bird that was always there was the olive thrush. He was just as territorial as the robin. We called him Fat Man because of his portly waddle: he loved to rootle about in the leaf-mould at the shady end of the garden, far too occupied with his own affairs to squabble with the robin. He was handsome and benign, a little corpulent – but not to be trifled with. He had just the slightest condescension to the smaller flocking birds that clamoured round the limestone bird bath.

He was in charge. He patrolled.

Elsewhere, but rarely out of sight, the robin bobbed and flirted, sang and darted, brighter, busier and more efficient than the rest – the doves and the sparrows, the bulbuls and canaries.

The thrush and the robin lived in a sort of independent harmony – like Hopie and Jumbie.

There were always people in the house. Hopie gathered to her every sort of person. Children, workers, waifs and strays; society ladies and local housewives. She had patience with everyone, turned nobody away. There was something in her face – not of kindliness alone, but of action and efficiency. Whether standing in a crowded street, racing down the aisles inside a shop, the lost or bewildered would always pick her out to ask a question, solicit help, beg for money, beg for bread. The curmudgeonliest of men lapped up her every word, the insecure and awkward hovered near her, talking earnestly; the gallant courted her with old-world honour and no expectation of reward.

Other women trusted her – with their children, with themselves.

At home the phone never stopped ringing – two longs, two shorts of the party line, whirring out of the box-phone on the wall. And there would be someone asking for a lift, a loan, a favour. Here, our neighbour, Phyllis, a little the worse for wear at ten in the morning and still in bed, the phone to her ear, an ashtray full of butts on the quilt beside her, begging a new box of cigarettes and a gossip – she with her wild intelligence and crackling humour, her gravel voice and ginger hair.

Hopie always went when she called, slipping through the stile between our gardens.

Tea and brown bread and butter were restoratives: for sadness, sickness or rash indulgence. She would get Phyllis up, make the tea, sit in the cool stone-walled living room, her legs tucked up beneath her and let Phyllis talk (mostly of what she had heard listening in on the party line) and take it away with her, unrepeatable and unrepeated.

Hopie never gossiped. It was something which she held as quite taboo – perhaps because she had been gossiped over once herself. Long ago, long before she came to be a robin in The Bush.

She always said to Nicky and me: discretion first, then kindness. And never talk about yourself unless you're pressed.

Sometimes Peggy Beeton would call – tinkling and musical – asking Hopie to bring her daughter Bessie back from school when she went for us. Hopie and Peggy were bosom friends and we would always stay for tea. The children were included, sitting at the veranda table – Nicky and Bessie and me. And little Doss, Bessie's younger brother, brought by Nursie from the garden.

What an occasion it always was! Proper cups of milky tea with sugar lumps served with tongs; slivers of toast spread with Little Man's Delight – Doss's name for Gentlemen's Relish

– or tiny sandwiches with sprigs of parsley popped between the slim triangles on a silver dish. Peggy would stretch out on the chaise longue in the shade of the creeper and I would gaze at her. I think she was the closest that one ever came to seeing the Queen. She was so astonishingly beautiful. Her hair, despite her youth, was silver-grey and smooth, her skin like a petal, her face finely sculpted round a slim patrician nose. She was tall and graceful as a heron and her voice was like a flute – always with a lilt of laughter and enquiry.

Hopie, who I usually considered the most Beautiful Person in the Universe, suddenly seemed just a little shabby: a paint stain on her slacks, her lipstick forgotten, her hair in a scarf, tackies on her feet because she had been hauling compost for the garden.

Nor did we match up, Nicky and I.

Shorts and shirts and sandals. That was it.

Hopie cut our hair far too carelessly and close, obviating nuisance.

Bess – the touchstone of all earthly aspirations and delights – had sprigged dresses with smocked yokes, red shoes with buttons and cardigans with small embroidered flowers. She could grow her hair to wear with a velvet Alice-band if she chose. She once had plaits with ribbons.

If I coveted her shoes (why did Hopie think red so unsuitable?), Bessie always asked to borrow my shorts when she came to play at our house and once Nicky cut her fringe with Hopie's sewing scissors, straight back from the brow, almost to the scalp. It was the only time I heard Peggy raise her voice or saw her angry. Bess was peremptorily hauled off home in the big black car in tears, little Doss trotting behind, giving her side-long glances of complicity: what impertinence and daring and delight!

Children never think that parents might have had another life: a history before they were born. A story or a secret.

Perhaps that is why Hopie seemed so much like the robin – concerned with the harmony of the garden and its occupants but keeping her counsel, her independence, her decisive discretion, her hidden nesting place.

It was a long winter afternoon and I was playing at Bess's house. Her elder brother Ben was home for the weekend from his prep school. Half in jest he set to hunting us, goading us to both delight and fright as we squealed and scattered.

I hid behind the heavy chintz curtains in the living room, creeping between the window seat and the back of the long sofa.

Footsteps came across the hall and I tucked myself down, barely breathing.

But it was not Ben in his big-boy shoes, making a threatening tramp, tramp, tramp. It was Peggy, floating in to fold herself and settle on the sofa, followed by a friend. I heard the cook bringing in the tea. The tinkle of the teacups, the chime of the thin silver spoons.

And the quiet voices, talking low.

I don't know what I heard that afternoon for no words could be reassembled when I sat alone and frightened with the dusty smell of the curtains, the silky green and burgundy tassel of the tie-back stringy in my sweaty grip. I only knew that something in my world had shifted.

Irrevocably.

Bessie found me later when the grown-ups had gone. 'Why did you spoil the game?'

'No one came to find me.'

'You shouldn't have hid away so much.' Crossly. 'Why do you *always* hide away?'


Do I?

That evening I went into the bathroom at home with its huge tub and its dark green concrete floor, its stiff taps and its loaf of Lifebuoy soap, saying nothing, shutting the door which I had never done before.

Hopie came to find me.

'What happened to you in the War?' I said.

'Lots of things.'

'Peggy said . . .'

Wary. 'What did Peggy say?'

'I can't remember.'

Only I could – but I did not know the meaning of the words except that somehow they were connected with an old photo album which Hopie kept at the bottom of her sewing drawer and into which I'd once looked when I was searching for string.

Hopie in her uniform, her WAAF's cap jaunty on her glossy head, her Captain's pips on her shoulders, her glorious, laughing gaze.

Instinct is a current: a strange alertness. Unexpected and unexplained.

There was a picture of a pilot with his wings on his chest and his rows of ribbons.

His eyes looked straight into mine.

Under the picture was a word: *Rex.*

Hopie lifted me out of the water and wrapped a towel around me and held me close. 'Come to the fireplace,' she said and she took me through, scooping my flannel pyjamas from beneath my pillow as we passed our room. Nicky was stretched out on the rug reading a book, twisting her finger round and round in a thick strand of dark, straight hair. Ninngy was knitting and clicking her teeth: click-click-click – the needles and the dentures. The small shift and flare of the logs settling in the grate, Brownie, the dachsie, twitching in her sleep, steaming slightly in the firelight. Jumbie was busy with the newspaper, his whisky in the heavy glass he always used resting on the arm of his chair.

I stood in front of the great open fireplace in the half-light to be rubbed to warmth, pyjama jacket lifted over my head, the stiff pants crackling quietly as I pushed my legs down into them. Hopie with the light behind her, the halo flare around her, her face in shadow.

'You are much prettier than Peggy,' I said. 'Even after everything she said.'

Hopie cut me short with a laugh: a robin flitting deftly out of reach. 'No one is prettier than Peg.'

That was true of course. But I said instead, 'No, you are prettier.'

Jumbie thumped his glass gently against the armrest, 'Quite right.'

A glance passed fleetingly between them.

Jumbie rattled his papers, got up, patrolling. He twitched the curtains to see that the windows behind them were closed, checked the front door, wound the clock.

Hopie drew me onto her lap.

Safe – for now.

There is always a robin in my garden. And a thrush. I see them every day and I remember: discretion was the virtue Hopie taught, loyalty the lodestar of Jumbie's life.

Here is the Fat Man thrush – dart and thrust, stop and check, dart and thrust again – marching along the edges of the lawn. And here is robin, busy with keeping order in the beds, singing from a different perch: its laughter and its morning song.

And even yet, after all these years of searching, I have never found its nest.

## CHAPTER FIVE
## *Swallows*

*U*celizapholo – that which asks a little milk.

When the cattle return to the byre at night they are accompanied by swallows and swifts, hunting the green dusk for the insects stirred up by passing hooves. They skim the backs of the milk cows and their chitter is the plaint that the herdboys should apportion them the last drop of milk before the udders empty.

It is the name, too, for the evening star which lights the herd to byre: *that which asks a little milk*. The star – the last trembling creamy drop glistening in the sky, the swallows, its emissaries in the dusk.

My earliest remembrance of swallows is their nesting in the living room of an old settler house. It was a thick-walled cottage said to have been built in the early 1800s with small windows, deep sills and a floor made of yellowwood planks. The eaves were shallow and so the swallows, welcome guests, nested inside. The occupants did not seem to mind the scattering of droppings from such propitious guests.

It was enchanting to watch them come and go so deftly and to hear, distinctly, the hungry fledglings in the chamber. There was something mysterious in the shadowy room because of them, a hushed respect for their presence: no one moved fast or spoke too loudly.

The house belonged to the manager of a small farm which was owned by titled industrialists and used as a country retreat. It was only twenty miles from town. Because of his work in selling earth-moving equipment, Jumbie knew the manager well.

Jumbie, so upright, so bluff, so much the war veteran, was doing a job (I find, in retrospect) far beneath his abilities. He felt it and bridled under its indignities. A major in the Air Force, a decorated veteran of the North African campaign, recipient of the OBE whose achievements have only emerged in recent years in the published memoirs of airmen, travelled through the Eastern Cape farming districts selling earth-moving equipment for a multinational. He had wanted to be an engineer – but when he applied at university he was scornfully rejected as being unfit for the task.

He had only one arm.

He had lost the other in an accident as a child.

It was a bitter blow. The lack of a limb seemed to presage a lack of intellect and competence.

The war rectified that score.

He could have avoided military service altogether but instead, enlisted in the Air Force, was commissioned, rose quickly to the rank of Major and was famed for getting equipment through to the squadrons under immensely difficult circumstances. His meticulous attention to daily detail, his ledgers and his tax files were still testimony to this old efficiency.

And good form in all he did and said.

The quintessential public schoolboy without the public school.

Which was another of his disappointments.

So we visited the manager instead of the titled people in the house, going down the bumpy road to the old tin-roofed dwelling, nesting in the deep shade beneath the spreading cobalt-shadowed branches of wild figs, the smell of rotting fruit faint on the air.

The manager was big and blond and friendly, tender to his wife – and his swallows. I, sitting quietly, watched those birds in their comings and goings, their trusting flutters and swoops above our heads as we had tea. I sensed the gentleness and serenity of the manager's wife, her coiled dark hair, her quiet smile as if she were there in direct communion with the birds – and he allowed them for her sake.

Far outside, commanding the view, the owner's house stood on its hillside, bright with lights at dusk as we went home. Another world without the rustle of wings.

'Of course, she's Australian,' Hopie said, glancing up at the lighted windows as we passed along the perimeter of the lawn. 'And they are all descended from convicts.'

Which put the lid on it.

Money didn't count – only breeding!

I never thought to question this quaint logic then.

It was only later that I knew that other house as well – with its pastel rooms, its gracious furniture, the library with its walls of leather-bound books, its occasional tables ranked with English magazines and bowls of flowers.

I came there as a teenager, a sort of hanger-on to a house party of well-known friends. A transient girlfriend.

Except I wasn't – and I'm still not allowed to forget that I'd once gone down the Bumpy Road to the manager's cottage! Or the comment overheard from the lady of the house (despite her Australian connections) to make my ears burn and my new, silky-pink bell-bottom suit feel suddenly like a librarian's tweed skirt and jumper, 'A blue-stocking, my dear. Most unattractive.'

I never ventured down the clipped swathe of lawn towards the manager's house when I was there. I did not glance at it or admit to the others of ever having been there years ago. But, in the noise of a tennis afternoon with the hi-fi blaring, I knew that it was somewhere down beyond the hedge where the pool of wild figs nestled in a fold between the slopes of hillside. I wondered if the people I had met so long ago still lived there then: she with her quiet gestures, her slender reach, waiting poised for swallow-flight.

I see them now – and am ashamed.

## CHAPTER SIX
## *Hoopoes and Drongos*

*H*oopoes are summer birds: coming to the lawn in the mornings when the sun is hot, the undulating dip of their flight, the sudden black and white, the rust-brick red of them and somewhere, nearby, the drongo in the tree, waiting to dart down, a wing, fanned grey, to thieve whatever the patient hoopoe has pulled from the earth.

'Those dratted drongos,' Ninngy used to say. She was incensed by their injustice.

Just as she was incensed when Harold Wilson won the British elections for Labour and ousted the Tories.

'Oh no, Hopie,' she cried in dismay. 'We can't have Labour.'

There would be a slide into anarchy and Empire had been betrayed.

She was gloomy for a week until the new crop of snapdragons and baby larkspur coming into flower drew her attention away from Westminster and kept her in the garden from dawn to dusk, the long, rangy, silent James Raga her constant shadow with the hosepipe or the barrow or the hoe.

I did not often play there when the whole procession of pets was wandering about in James and Ninngy's wake. The hoopoes kept away as well and only the olive thrush was busy at the edges of the garden rustling up the dead twigs and grass. The hoopoes took themselves off to the quiet, dusty shade of the fields, probing the ridges where the mealies grew. The drongos followed, perching and darting at them from the shrubs that edged the land.

I would find a pair of hoopoes secretive together, suddenly camouflaged by the latticework of shadow from the mealie leaves, despite their bold black and white and russet marking. They were the last birds seen before the cultivation gave way to the deep bush, its silence – but for the furtive rustle of a small brown bird – limpid in the filtered light. Hoopoes were never found in this deep bush. They lived at the littoral edges of thicket and cultivation. They liked the furrowed rows, turned up by the hoe in this outlying mealie land.

The path to it wound through thorn bush, ending in a gate. It was a spiteful gate, difficult to open, strung too tight and made of slim poles linked by barbed wire. It had to be dragged between the gate posts so that the wire hoop would reach the hasp. It was easier to crawl under it than try to open it.

There were different types of gates at Penderley, each with its particular character. There were stile gates which did not need to be opened but which kept bush pigs and buck at bay and heavy pole and iron-rung gates which were laborious to open: each pole had to be shifted aside. But they were perfect to climb on and to use as a gym bar, to balance on, toes pointed like a dancer. They were sturdy gates that would keep a blundering bull at bay or a high-treading stallion like the Hopes, whose prancing hooves chopped alarmingly as he made rushes at the fence, stopping short, sending up the dust.

Those five-barred gates divided the world into garden, pasture, paddock and beyond with the white lime road threading down between the different properties. Climbing over them gave a sense of change, of passage from one precinct to another and guided the choice of voice to be used: boisterous or laughing, secretive or silent. Each place had its language.

The mealie field where the hoopoes probed and pottered was a place for quiet voices. Sometimes James Raga would be there working between the rows with his hoe. He rarely spoke to anyone. In this part of the property – alone – he smoked. Something he never did when he worked with Ninngy. Here he *skoffelled* deftly with his hand-rolled newspaper stub between his lips, one eye closed to a slit against the drift of smoke. The smell of it is still familiar. The sweet, distinctive scent of dagga.

I remember Hopie saying once, 'James, *jy's 'n dagga-roker. Ek weet dit.*'

And he replying, '*Dagga, missis? Wat is dagga?*'

It was dagga that was his downfall. And the *skokiaan* he made from brown bread and pineapple in the square drums that held the paraffin we used for lighting lamps.

Raging drunk and dagga-dazed, he killed his wife Katie.

It was not long after their wedding, despite the five children that lived with them in the tiny house that we had built for staff.

That wedding, caught on cine camera by Hopie, was held in the schoolhouse chapel with the Reverend Msizi officiating. The bridal party had proceeded down the road with whoops and ululations to our gate, been silent and decorous on our lawn for pictures. Katie wore a wide, white satin dress. A square of lace which Hopie had bought for her was balanced on her head like a doily on a jug, rather stiff and catching at an angle on her woolly hair. She had a face that was crumpled with toil, a ribald face, her front teeth missing, subdued that day into dignity, no cackle-laugh which I had so often heard, like a raucous chicken pursued by the cock, half affronted, half expectant. She carried frangipani from our tree and some plastic flowers which Hopie had once owned and then discarded – pink cherry blossom from Japan, stiff and dusty.

Their children, starched, scrubbed and carrying prayer books, followed on behind, grinning and shyly strutting for Hopie's lens, astounded into silence by the Polaroid snap which emerged from Basil Brody's camera and which he presented to James like a conjuror producing a rabbit from a hat.

James was kitted out in Jumbie's old suit. Wraith-thin, it was far too big for him but he had that face, that distant view of things, a pastoralist looking out over hills for his cattle, a fine, chiselled aquiline nose, a nineteenth century painting, despite the shabby jacket – idealised, contemplative and beautiful.

Except for his eyes.

They were yellow from the dagga and hostile to the world.

We had watched the bridal party go, followed by the rag-tag of all The Bush, dressed for the occasion, weaving ceremoniously past the coal shed and vegetable garden, down through the paddock to the Ragas' house for a more traditional feast which went on late into the night. Faintly came the sound of drumming as if a cardboard box had been appropriated for the task and singing, rich and plaintive, night birds calling after moonrise.

Not long afterwards, Katie Raga was dead.

No one told us how. Or why.

–Don't tell the children.

But one night there were murmurs from beyond the kitchen door, hurrying feet, a voice raised then lowered swiftly, the sound of a car coming down the drive: a bobbing police van shouldering its way along the track to the stable paddock. Torchlight.

–Don't tell the children.

But Nicky found out because she always listened when the grown-ups talked even though she seemed to be absent.

–He caught her with another man, down in the mealie field.

–How do you mean, caught her?

–You know.

–Know what?

Nick just rolled her eyes and went away.

But that explained the newly dug grave at the bottom of that selfsame mealie field where the hoopoes came. The white-painted cross.

Katie was buried where she'd died. The soil was mounded up, full of large, striped snail shells. Creeping weeds seeded themselves on the sandy hump of earth.

James Raga disappeared for six months.

He was in North End jail where the stink of the carbon factory lingers even in a howling gale, where the primitive vegetation in the graveyard is blasted flat and leans with the prevailing wind and the blind windows stare out across the railyards and wetlands where the wheeling seabirds flock.

A crime of passion, extenuating circumstances, diminished responsibility: his sentence was a gesture by the Court.

Months after his release, he was arrested for stealing one of the Morelands' sheep and was sentenced to six years for stock-theft.

Hopie was incensed. How could James Raga get six years for stock-theft and six months for culpable homicide? Even in extenuating circumstances. It showed the value that the State accorded women in comparison with sheep!

It was Ninngy who insisted James came back on his release. 'Well, Hopie, what about his children?' she had simply said.

So the family reappeared: thin, wild, older and bedraggled from a long sojourn with relations. James Raga worked the garden as before, he and Ninngy wordless in their quiet communication. It bloomed as always – out of the fine black sand and drought-raddled thorn, the English flowers tender and unblemished under his sinewy black hands.

And in the field, when slipping past to take the path down to my favourite milkwood hidden in a clearing in the bush, I might find him digging in between the rows of mealies. Once I saw him standing by the grave, his hand on his hoe, so still that a hoopoe in the shade kept probing gently at the earth under the sweet thorn at its head.

I went away, backing down the path and slipping under the gate. Fleetingly, I sensed the burden of a life, maimed beyond my understanding. But I knew why Ninngy had no fear of him and why she sheltered him. In her simple way, belief stood firm against the prejudice and opportunism of the world: its judges, its governments – its drongo birds.

**CHAPTER SEVEN**

*Paradise Flycatcher*

T he flycatcher had nested in my secret tree. Such a wonder of a nest, dappled with pale green lichen, the small sea-salt tendrils of old man's beard deftly woven into a cone, so perfectly camouflaged within the whiskery branches.

Climbing there one day I saw him with his long rusty tail. The dip of his flight, the dark eye, the fragment of ochre-red among the dark green leaves. Then I heard his song.

There is nothing so like a secret rippling laugh. So rarely heard. And so particular.

It was a privilege that he had chosen my tree and his nest was far enough away from the bole and the long branch on which I used to perch that I did not disturb him, only saw the flash of him when he came to perch on its rim.

*Jejane, Jejane,*

*Uhleka ntoni na?*

*Jejane, Jejane,*

*At what are you laughing?*

It was Hopie who first told me the little bird's name. She had seen one in the syringa tree outside her bedroom window one morning and exclaimed and pointed, drew me close to look, wriggled in that way she always did when she was excited and said, 'What a happy thing. I hope it will nest there.'

It chose my tree instead.

I do not recall Hopie ever coming to my tree. There were places on the plot which were out of bounds to adults and, it seems, this had been respected. Perhaps it was busyness and preoccupation rather than restraint for I would never have wished her away.

For me, that tree was a solitary place, a place of grey dappled bark and a great clump of mistletoe in a fork in the bole, of the sparkle of new waxy leaves in sunlight and the faintest rustlings in the surrounding bush. It was from here that my friend Lesley-Jean and I could look out across the bush to the faraway stain of the sea and from where we used to launch our expeditions over the bush-covered dunes. We never asked permission to go nor seemed to cause any anxiety at home. Looking back, it is surprising – the risk of snakebite, of stumbling on snares, of meeting vagrants in the clearings was real.

Such dangers did not concern us. We had no fear that we might get lost though the paths were faint and only used by game or poachers pushing their way through to set their wire traps.

We were intent on treasure – and treasure there was!

This stretch of coastal bush with its alien thickets of Port Jackson willow had once been the site of the city dumps a hundred years before. They were long abandoned, long overgrown with thorn and brush. But we discovered two sites where the waste of a century lay half-buried in the bush and held all the fascination of an archaeologist's dig.

Here were ginger beer jars and water bottles, their necks moulded round crusty green marbles. Here were old kettles, their enamel chipped off, their spouts crooked. Here were toothpaste containers made of porcelain. One, perfectly preserved, crested with the Lion and the Unicorn, was inscribed:

*Oriental Tooth Paste*

*For Cleansing and Beautifying*

*And Preserving the Teeth and Gums*

There were jars which once contained cold cream and small brown-fluted medicine bottles. And once, a tiny porcelain baby, no doubt the inmate of a long-forgotten doll's house. Without clothes, with one leg missing and the paint bleached from her face, I carried her home in my pocket along with a more recent yellow shoe – high-heeled and platformed with a peep toe and a thin buckled ankle-strap. I put it on the pelmet above my window along with a collection of oil flasks and ginger beer jars.

Some time later someone swept my treasures away. No one warned me or asked me if I minded. They were 'dust-collectors' and the shoe a 'smelly old wreck', the novelty of which I was sure to have 'got over'. No one knew that lying in the dark, looking up at it, I had so often imagined that shoe and its canary-yellow mate tripping down Main Street from Garlicks to Cleghorns, accessory to a smart town suit with velvety lapels and covered buttons. Wasp waist, long throat, sheer seamed stockings. Such a story it had to tell, so confident and sure: a tiptoe-shoe for kissing!

I think the shoe and the bottles were all thrown into the deep well-shaft in the paddock where a windmill had once stood. The lips of the hole were overhung with thick Kikuyu grass and everything went down there which was not destined for the compost heap.

My pelmet was well dusted and the curtain frill was crisp and neat again.

It was not long after this that Les and I abandoned exploring the dumps. And then I stopped going down to the milkwood where the flycatcher nested and from which I could see right across the bush to the sea beyond.

Les didn't come that often any more – she took more avidly to riding horses and I, in turn, became afraid of them. I spent my time, instead, on the roof of the garage, writing foolish love stories and poems in a secret book.

So the transference of place became a rite of passage: climbing trees was childish; climbing ladders to brood in the shade of the water tank was something of a tryst.

And it was.

For I was not alone: I was conjuring heroes.

Bomber pilots, naval officers, great white hunters, soldiers, poets: all tall, dark and handsome, with blazing blue eyes (the result of listening to radio serials on Friday nights) – and Elgar playing in the background (even if I didn't recognise his music then).

But the real heroes of my life have been of a very different cast. One composed a poem for me – a praise in the Zulu-style, the metaphor of bird for man, nature personified: the flycatcher and myself.

*Jejane, Jejane, intokazi.*

*Dearest one*

If, to me, it seemed an unlikely metaphor, it was a tender gift. And it recalled, at once, that secret rippling laugh, the tiny silvery bell of enchantment that I had once heard so long ago in my milkwood, the flash of ochre-red, the dusky crest, the cryptic nest of lichen and clematis, the wakening green of spring. It recalled the moment of setting off on an adventure in search of treasure.

In this lay the aptness of its delight.

Years later I sometimes saw poor woodcutters at the side of the road selling sacks of brushwood and, set out on the gravel verge, small offerings scrounged from those long-forgotten dumps. It was a time when cottage bric-a-brac was fashionable and every student like myself had a bunch of grasses in a ginger beer crock or a flower in a discarded apothecary's jar.

*Morris's Imperial Eye Ointment*

*Infallible cure for all diseases*

*Of the eyes*

In time they went out of fashion as collectables and disappeared with the roadside hawkers and their donkey carts and sacks of brush. That stretch of road is fenced now and bristles with rusty razor-wire: a new hostility and wariness.

And in our valley someone bought the plot below our paddock and built a vast Tuscan-style house: columns, distressed paintwork and a vibracrete fountain recycling water through the urn held on the shoulder of a moulded fibreglass goddess. The ripple-laugh of the flycatcher is replaced by the relentless tinkle of chlorinated water: round and round and round.

I cannot tell if my tree is still at the edge of the landscaped garden. Those that have remained seem dwarfed by the bulk of the building. Or perhaps I have simply grown taller.

And the numinous has become prosaic: not in itself – but in my heart.

**CHAPTER EIGHT**

*Spreeus*

*Witgat spreeus*, redwinged starlings, pied starlings. The proletariat of birds. The mobs and masses. Flocking birds which lose, by their habit, the mark of individuality. And yet, there is no more poignant sound on an autumn day than the melancholic murmur of redwinged starlings – a gentle sough in trees, far outside the busyness of mornings, an undertow of loss. I remember them beyond the classroom window in the winter term. They were the harmony to homesickness, the longing to walk away. I would see them about the playing fields – the red blur of them in flight, the glossy purple and the ashen mauve of their heads, deep-piled as velvet: midnight colours, richer than plum.

*Spreeus* are the noisy ones, the ragamuffin flocks, garrulous and brash. In many ways we children in The Bush were like a gang of *spreeus* flocking from house to house, foraging here and there for food, clattering our roller skates across the iron grids to whizz down the road when it had been newly tarred, Nicky and Steffi Brody at the front, Bessie and me trailing far behind, not intrepid enough to get up speed.

The best house to go to was the Brodys. It was a squabble-kingdom where no one interfered. The Brody parents, Basil and Elspeth, were at their bookshop, and Miriam was in the kitchen – too thin, too spare, too preoccupied (she with a face wrinkled as a *gaukum* fig) to bother with the things we did.

Here, indeed, was a place to forage.

It was the most exciting kitchen in the The Bush. Not by its appointments but by the treasures in the larder cupboard. Ancient, dusty, with foreign labels and covered with rust spots: shrimps and anchovies, scallops and oysters, boxes of prawn chips which fizzed up into pale green and pink petals when tossed in hot oil. There were slabs of Bourneville chocolate and a big bin of treacle sugar which we used for making toffee.

An old striped curtain was looped up in front of the cupboard, the rows of small Coca Cola bottles in their crate squatted on the floor. We were allowed whatever we liked – there was no one to object.

This was not a house for one-mint-lump-after-lunch and one-square-of-chocolate- after-supper measured out by Ninngy.

We fell on the feast like a bunch of greedy birds, squabbling over the best bits, Steff directing with her gruff voice, the little ones pecking and fluttering and overturning the sugar. Toast was made from white bread sliced very thin. Butter melted in puddles and dripped through onto grubby fingers; plump pink prawns curled among the crumbs. We licked our plates happily, left them scattered about the counter. Outside, Miriam washed dishes in an old paraffin tin with cold water taken from the pump, her bare feet wide-toed and prehensile, her arms wet above the elbows as she drifted her eyes over us, across the garden, seeking some other spot of reference. I never remember hearing her talk until the day she squawked like a chicken and ran shrilly back to the kitchen, '*Pofadder! Kom gou!*' and we gathered round just as shrilly, chattering like startled starlings as a great, slack, gravid female was hooked by the gardener from the moonflower that grew outside the bedroom door.

'It's all those cats,' Ninngy used to say. 'That's what brings the snakes!' And she clicked her dentures, shifting them back and forth briefly. 'It's not right to let them breed that way.'

'Well, they *are* Catholics,' Hopie murmured wryly.

The Brodys had dozens of cats – and, by 'Bush standards', dozens of children. Kittens tumbled about in doorways, their sires and dams lay carelessly along the edge of the water tank. They crept off, half alert, half sulky on approach. Grey tabbies, amber-eyed, thin and fierce. Only the Persian stayed indoors, the real pet, flat-faced and sour.

No one paid any of them the least attention.

Having eaten, we played dress-up with the 'King Kong Box'. It was full of cocktail frocks, old bags, ancient shoes and a high-collared, regal velvet cloak. Everyone had their part in a game: Steff the king, Nicky the queen, Tessa Brody the princess because she was blonde and small and compliant. Bess was the woodcutter or the baby or the wicked godmother – just depending. I can't remember what I was. Maybe the orphan: a certain histrionic melancholy of which I am ashamed!

Boy Brody never played. He was off in the bush with a catty, overwhelmed by the presence of four sisters and their friends. He would not be cajoled into being a villain or a victim – or even a prince.

Sometimes there were more of us – town girls, brought home from school. Then, something subtle changed. A certain swagger and propriety overcame the older ones and we, the younger, were pushed out, pecked at with scorn. No longer useful to the game.

I have seen *spreeus* attack a weaker bird, turning on it – mob-madness: such sharp-eyed cruelty.

Ours was not the only cruelty connected with the lives of *spreeus*. We, half in jest – and spite and silliness – knew the hierarchy (and boundaries) of the games that usually end in triumph or in tears.

But there was a deeper hurt that we, as girls, were spared.

Perhaps that's why Boy Brody – patronised, even in his name, by bossy condescension – took himself off, weary of us and our constant squabbling, knowing something we did not.

Small boys, at the boys-only prep school, were required to wear a tie with the school colours designating House: red for Hoopoes, green for Kingfishers. But there was a dirty grey-blue tie kept as punishment for 'bad boys', brought from the teacher's cupboard on occasion, as deadly as the hangman's hood.

The recipient was known as a *spreeu*.

It announced a filthy boy, a bed-wetter, a dunce who did not know his work, blotted his books, forgot his pens, failed his tests, an outcast from the class. He was 'marked' by boys and staff alike.

Little Grimes II, six years old, was a constant *spreeu*. Perhaps it was his snotty nose, perhaps the blue-tinged kneecaps which offended or the crusty eyes, glued from sleeplessness and crying. Sent from farm to boarding school, his was a bewildering world. Like the other boys – unfed, hungry, he fluttered aimlessly behind them as they flocked, searching for extra food, scouring the garden and bush around the grounds for *dinnebessies*, *droog-my-keel*, cabbage stalks, lemon rind, the fatty rumps of flying ants whenever they swarmed. The fine array of art books, the prints of famous paintings, the concertos played on the wind-up gramophone on

Sunday evenings, did not compensate any of them for their hunger and homesickness.

Right down the pecking order in terms of age, ability and stamina, Grimes II wore his *spreeu*-tie like a manacle around his neck: the butt of jokes and scorn and misdirected, boyish rage.

Grimes II: the first remembered cog in any Old Boy's worn nostalgia. He was good reason to believe why being 'brought up tough' is 'always good for you'.

No one knows what happened to Grimes II.

He grew up, dropped his 'minor' designation when his brother left the school, swapped his place in the relentless chain and graduated into manhood.

Perhaps he thought that being brought up tough was good for him as well.

Or perhaps he didn't.

Who knows what mobbing *spreeus* mean to Mr Grimes now.

## CHAPTER NINE
## *Hawks*

*A*lfred Banda came from Nyasaland. How he arrived here, so far from home, the circumstances of his journey, the reason for his choice, I do not know. Certainly, he had been here a long time for he spoke Xhosa to the others. Whether he was fluent, if he had an accent, how he was perceived, I could not tell but for many years he worked in our house where other men, traditionally, refused to enter.

All around The Bush, families like the Morelands and the Beetons employed men in the house. Imports from the 'Federation', they had a colonial cachet, spruce in their white uniforms and starched aprons but it was only the Beetons who togged their man out in a red sash to wait at table and taught him to chauffeur a car.

Alfred Banda was about forty. He was very dark, his skin the hue of a blue-black *isipingo* berry, quite different from James Raga or the Djantjes. His hair was dressed up into a cone at the front – it gave him stature, height and presence. I decided he was a chief, a man who wore leopard skins or loped along in search of game, graceful as an antelope. There was a world in his gestures.

When Nicky and I were small and ate in the kitchen at the rush table set close to the Aga stove, Alfred Banda, preparing the evening meal, would tell us stories. I do not know what language he spoke for it was incomprehensible to us and even to Jane Djantjes who listened as she washed the dishes. I only know that they were about Hare and Tortoise from Alfred's imitations: head alert, eyes starting, whiskers a-tremble or the ponderous gait of Tortoise, his beaky mouth munching fallen flowers.

So apt, so exact.

I recall the tremulous accents of the hare, the low sonorous voice of the tortoise, the jinks and leaps of one, the other overturned, stump legs in the air. All this accompanied by a high sing-song, the voice particular and thrilling.

The stories always took place once the lamps were lit and our boiled egg and bread fingers were set before us on the pale green plates. The wicks of the lamps hissed blue with a flare of orange and a drift of charcoal-coloured fumes. The shadows of those lamps loomed large and smoking against the whitewashed walls: they were votive candles in a tabernacle, they sent strange flares of light across Alfred Banda's face, a shaman in a trance. He was ready to deliver an *isanqa* – his fantastical story, his 'halo around the moon'.

Rapt, we listened as if waiting for some distant thunder.

At the last he turned into a monster – half toad, half manikin, sinister and swift. He would crouch, knees akimbo, hands placed between his feet to balance and then propel himself around the room on his haunches, deft as a lizard, pirouetting on a whim to terrify his watchers, only the whites of his eyes showing and his lids turned inside out so they seemed to glow red.

Jane Djantjes, watching with us – merry Jane, tiptoe-dancing Jane, and all a-twinkle with the tiny earrings in her ears – would shriek then, laughter gone, throw her apron over her eyes, trembling and crying all at once and we – afraid – would rush behind her and cling to her skirts.

But how we loved it!

How we loved the sounds, those trills and grunts and exclamations, that pantheon of little animals: the trusting and the sly, the buffoons and the wily, the praised and the derided. They were there – and, if absorbed by sound and fright and laughter, I recognised them later when I came to learn about them and their provenance, reading old forgotten books of anthropology in a cavernous library.

In knowing them I understood that Alfred Banda, in this peri-urban wilderness of flat grey bush, plots and creeping urban sprawl nudging at the edges of my protected little paradise, had gone in search of childhood. Through us, he was reaching for a past long left behind.

He was the man whose heart 'returns again to dig in the deserted village', some half-mythic homestead in a Land of Punt which he had lost.

I owe to him the knowledge of 'the gesture' – that primal benediction of the storyteller before words bring forth the characters from shadow. Those creatures which he conjured to inhabit my childhood world are with me still and bird and animal and plant retain their deep connection to the mythic mind: an old cosmology, a different cadence, a love of language where alliteration is the song of the soul.

*Kwasukasukelwa* – Once upon a time.

It was because of him.

*Kanti* – and even yet.

So was the natural world defined: for through him my heart opened to a world both numinous and apt. Just as stars in the sky cannot go by prosaic scientific designations and retain their intimacy, so are the months and seasons named for their winds and birds, their flowers blooming or fading, their trees budding, young life burgeoning: *'it is the season of the reedbuck lambs'; 'it is the ripening of the millet'; 'it is the time for lighting fires in the hearth'.*

The wind, too, became a harbinger – just as the birds or stars or trees were known. I love the *bergwind* more than anything: the heat of it, the edge of fire and fear. It comes from beyond the mountains, from the dry wastes and empty watercourses. It is a great bird which lives in a cave in the mountains: the warmth of its armpit, the heat of its eye, the swift, hot sweep of its scything wing. This is what makes the *boerboon* leaves fold flat, the *witgat* tremble, the gwarri brace its claw to rock.

When the red-chested cuckoo shouts it is time to put the hoe on the shoulder, when the hadedas cry clamorously, there will be a good harvest. When the black korhaan heralds in the dawn, it will be a windy day. Here is the red-fronted tinker barbet, *unoqand'ilanga*, striker-of-the-sun, beating his relentless little anvil in the deeper bush, gonging in the dun, the molten iron of summer. Here is the Jacobin cuckoo who cries in the autumn, '*Khawula, khawula, khawula*. Halt your work! It is time to harvest.'

In our bush lived *ubikwe*, Burchell's coucal, known as 'the bow of the gods', delivering his soft adagio of falling notes, foretelling rain. A woodwind bird, in minor key. Here is the greybacked cisticola that chimes the dusk on misty days when the setting sun cannot be seen. It is the bush-clock, marking the hours.

July will always be the month of aloes, *Eyentlaba*, for they bloom among the ironstone, candlelit against the cold blue blaze of winter skies. September brings the spring with the blooming of the erythrina with its crisp, curved petals, the red of blanket-clay. March is the time when the kites gather in the high winds of late summer, conferring for the great migration north.

One year Alfred Banda went away, like a migrating hawk.

He did not return for two years.

Then one day he simply reappeared unexpectedly, wearing a suit and two-tone shoes, a pair of dark glasses and his hair, that noble crest, was flattened, parted and slicked with Brylcreem.

'Oh dear,' said Ninngy. 'Is he a *tsotsi*?'

'Of course not!' Hopie's quiet reproof. 'The Nyasas have their independence now. He simply has the vote.'

Jumbie said he had become 'a Commie'. The sunglasses were a sure sign of sedition.

–What's a Commie?

–Never mind.

Nicky thought he looked cool.

So did the young women in The Bush. He had a transistor radio and a way of walking with it perched on his shoulder like a bird.

He did not stay long after that.

One day he was gone and I don't think I even said goodbye. Perhaps I was off exploring the bush and Alfred Banda's room was closed, a new brass padlock hanging on the hasp. We no longer had a man in a white suit cooking in the kitchen. I think we slipped a notch or two in the hierarchy of 'Bush families' with only Jane Djantjes singing at the sink and doubling up uproariously whenever she was amused – full of magpie laughter.

They say that the hawks gather before their long migration home in their sleek, fierce finery, always on a day of high dust and wind, rising – higher, higher, higher – high above the pestilence of air to circle, to salute, to drift suddenly from sight.

I often wondered where Alfred Banda was, his clan name the same as that of his new President. I wondered if he remembered us or if he soon forgot – as carelessly as we had seemed to do ourselves.

But I did not forget. And my cosmology is born of his.

If mine is muddled, mingled, half-distilled and re-concocted as a way of apprehending beauty in the world, I know that it began from the stories which he dredged up from his exile's heart, *umzwangedwa*, the grief which one feels alone: the bird of the windy hillside, the wanderer searching through the ash heaps of those long-deserted kraals.

I hope that he went home.

# CHAPTER TEN
## *Bee-Eaters*

*T*hey came at Christmas Time, announcing themselves by the high, sweet, joyful note of return. 'The bee-eaters are back!' Hopie would exclaim and she would always stop the car to look at them when we passed the cutting where they nested in a limestone bank at the edge of the road that led down to the beach. They were the birds of the long holidays, of summer, ebullient and vivid.

I did not know where ours came from. Some say from Russia and Eurasia and others that they were migrants from the far hinterland of Africa. They returned to our bank year after year. Suddenly, what was prosaic, dry and barren, backed by scrofulous grey gums and alien Port Jackson willow, took on a glamour through their sudden iridescent presence and the piercing sweetness of their call. When they were gone and summer drifted into autumn, spider webs closed the entrances to burrows and the bank became the haunt of mice and insects.

The bee-eaters were the harbingers of Christmas and its whitewashed tree, made from a dried thorn branch and festooned with cellophane streamers and ragged decorations. Nicky and I loved them, nonetheless, taking each from the old cardboard box into which they had been tossed the year before and restoring them to their festive glory. Nothing could be left off, no matter how burdened the branch. Artistry meant little in the need to give each ornament its place: I knew too well the sadness of being overlooked or thought not good enough to shine.

Our African tree was set in a bucket of sand in the living room and the round paint-chipped multicoloured lights festooned through the branches. It was ravishing when the generator worked and the small lights glowed – until the time I saw the Beetons' tree. That was a *proper* tree, symmetrical and spiky green – a fir – with tartan bows and lights that flickered on and off. It shimmered with perfectly enchanting rosy robins, painted angels and glass-fluted bells.

But Hopie would take no carping on the subject from Nicky or me. She insisted on an African tree: we did not live in England and fir trees were alien and boring. Perhaps she was right – but our knobbly branch with white-painted flakes of lichen and old man's beard had sword-sharp thorns that caught the streaming cellophane in a draught and hooked unwary passersby.

It was the time when Hopie did up parcels for the staff. I went with her to Bob's shop to buy sacks of mealie meal, packets of beans and great bottles of orange squash. The shop was near the bee-eaters' bank, hidden down a winding track, mostly used by donkey carts. It was a Cash Store with the words painted white on the faded red tin roof and Mrs Bob presided, dispensing tea and soap, paraffin and instant beer mix, bread and candles.

She was a ponderous, gentle widow with a grey bun pinned at her nape and she wore a cotton apron over her frock. Sometimes her daughter with the curly apricot-coloured plaits worked behind the counter in the holidays. I used to wonder if anyone ever came to play with her and her brother. They were so isolated in their clearing in the bush, so self-contained and quiet. So adult in the way they spoke, the dexterity with which they worked the till.

But if Bob's shop was the place for the farm workers and the woodcutters to pick through a knotted rag counting out flat bronze pennies, one by one, to buy a box of matches or a twist of sugar in a newspaper cone, it was, for us, an emporium of all the best delights imaginable. The counter was lined with large glass jars of sweets. Here were globular orange apricots – too sweet, too big and yet too tempting to resist. Here were blackjacks and pinkies and big square Wilson's toffees that took an afternoon to eat. Here were bulls' eyes and gobstoppers and flat khaki lozenges that burned and made our noses tingle into sneezes. There were small packets of fake cigarettes, heart-shaped love tokens which, for some reason, were usually printed in Afrikaans: '*Nie Sonder Jou*'. There were barley sugar sticks and – best of all – buttermilk suckers in pale pink gingham wrappers.

Hopie always bought brown bread and white – a loaf of each and put them on the back seat of the car and we, mouse-nibbling, excavated the loaf leaving the crust intact but the hot heart hollowed out. Even raging indigestion did not keep us from the feast. Hopie pretended to mind – but didn't. We all knew that bread and butter sprinkled with brown treacle sugar had been her favourite as a child. She spoke about it sometimes when we used to say, 'Tell us about being little.'

Then we heard about the bread and treacle sugar, tastier than any cake, smoking in the macrocarpa hedge and ice cream that her mother made from custard left to freeze in a bowl on the lawn when the heavy winter frosts came down. We knew all the flavours of her childhood – the figs, the quinces and the mutton chops grilled on a fire somewhere in the hills – she was so vivid and precise.

It made up for the dubious distinction of never having baked either Nicky or me a birthday cake. She was blithely unconcerned with cooking. Instead, Ninngy pottered in the kitchen, making Scotch baps or pancakes.

Nicky and I were not enthusiastic.

How much more exciting were the shop-bought chocolate éclairs at the Brodys which came in a box with *Lillwill's* printed in green across the front and a picture of a jolly chef in his high hat, or the little crispy cheese straws the Beetons always served on a starched and folded napkin in a silver dish, or Daniel Moreland's flaky scones with knobbly crusts.

There was something frugal about our kitchen – no waste, no self-indulgence. Something of the war-time ration book remained – ten years on – though strictly countered by the absence of certain things which reminded Hopie far too much of troop ships in convoy on the cold Atlantic. She would not tolerate Brussels sprouts. She had eaten them too often. And she always said, with a laugh, half teasingly, 'I decided if we were torpedoed I'd run a hot bath, get into it and drown in comfort.'

Ninngy, Scottish to the core, disapproved of 'fancy food' and Hopie was far too busy with a thousand projects to worry about what emanated from the kitchen. But to Jumbie, being served a plate of boiled potato and corned beef with mustard was the high point in his week. 'Ah, stovies, jolly good show!' he would exclaim heartily.

It was not a 'good show' to Nicky and me.

The blubber on the corned beef was as bad as the pimples on the blue-tinged ox tongue which came with raisin sauce as a special treat some Sundays. It was as suspect as the rice pudding curdled after days of neglect to a delicate sourness disguised by jam.

Oh, for the succulent medallions of meat at the Beetons with nutty nuggets of sautéed potato or the feast of tinned shrimps and Bourneville chocolate at the Brodys, washed down with Coke.

And yet, even these delights did not have quite the piquancy of a loaf of bread from Mrs Bob's, eaten secretly between us all crammed onto the back seat of the Morris Minor as Hopie drove us home from school.

Hopie was generous with her parcels for the staff. No matter how she 'counted pennies' she would make up cardboard cartons full of groceries and a few special treats for the children. Christmas meat gave off the odour of blood and brown paper for a few days in the bottom of the paraffin-fired fridge, resting in a white enamel baking tray to catch the drips.

James Raga liked a *kop en pootjies* for his feast – not a sheep's head but a pig's. I remember going with Hopie to the butcher in town, the sawdust on the floor, the excruciating wail of the saw as the butcher in his indigo and white-striped apron stood across a carcass and sawed and planed, wrapping the cuts deftly in brown paper. How I loved the quick slap and turn as he folded the paper in a single gesture – tying it with string, pushing the account slip under the knot and leaving a bloody fingerprint.

I stood transfixed beside Hopie, held by the glare of the pale-eyed pig's head on the slab, the straight white eyelashes, the rubbery snout. There it was, deposited on a sheet of newsprint, watching me. Beside it, disembodied, lay its trotters, four of them: petit-point ballerina pumps and just as pink.

James had his *kop en pootjies* boiled in an iron pot hour on hour while, under a bush, well hidden and covered with a lid of cardboard weighted with a stone, his honey, brown bread and pineapple brew fermented and frothed. Its effects – sampled like a connoisseur over days – ensured that the Aga stove in our kitchen was unattended. It became a matter of faith that the Aga (kept so constant over the year) would go out around Christmas from neglect, or flicker coolly, giving only enough heat for warming damp dish towels hanging on its rail.

And so our Christmas turkey was a pale bird, a touch pink and glutinous around the joints. Compensation came in the mountain of roast potatoes which Jane cooked in lard on a primus and the blue-flamed plum pudding with the tickeys hidden in its depths.

We always had the Christmas Eve Bush Party at our house, everyone bringing their basket of drinks and a plate of food. The feast was laid out on the dining room table with a sheet ironed stiffly as a cloth and bunches of red poinsettias to make it festive. Uncle Davey sat at the piano and played carols, Gramps blew on his penny-whistle with a coronet of tinsel round his head, his glasses as askew as the next whisky dictated. Jumbie was hearty and expansive to all, squirting soda from the siphon, splashing it into glasses rather recklessly as time went on. Hopie was all a-sheen with mystery and loveliness in her sweetheart neckline and the dip of her shining wing of hair. How Tom Moreland and Billy Beeton loved to pay her court. It was a marvel to observe.

We were sent to bed at ten. Ninngy tucked us up instead of Hopie. When she had gone, Nicky and I would creep out and sit, infuriated, at the other side of the passage door beyond which the riot escalated. We could hear the adults playing foolish games: charades and the young bucks pushing beer bottles about with their noses, racing for a finish line at the far end of the carpet, taking bets. We listened with alarm to the singing and dancing, whoops and gusts of laughter sweeping up the chimney and frightening away the Expected Midnight Visitor. We had both hung pillowcases by the grate in expectation.

If the people did not go, *he* would not come.

But in the morning, those pillow cases were always knobbly with parcels, the plate of biscuits on the mantelpiece was empty but for crumbs, the mug of beer half-drunk and other, foreign-looking parcels – including the big brown paper box with string and stamps which always came from Scotland – were piled beneath the Christmas tree.

Almost as soon as the tea tray was brought, the Djantjes and the Ragas would assemble outside the living room window and Jumbie, in his dressing gown – somewhat frayed himself – would hand out gifts, rather like a Rajah. One by one the children approached, the little ones holding back, hands together, bobbing a knee, eyes cast down.

Somehow I always hated that parade, even as a very small girl: the cheap sweets and bars of serviceable soap, the rag-tag, pot-luck bag of second-hand clothes. It made the promise of the crib in the limestone stable that Nicky and I had made, a lie. I knew it even if I didn't dare to say it. And I wanted them to go away, James herding them before him like a little flock of goats. I wanted them to go so the frightened flutter in my throat would disappear, my sweaty palms uncurl. If they did not go, how could I play with my toys in happiness, smelling of brand-new plastic and cellophane? How could I run about in rapture with those sad, dark eyes watching?

But it was a transient chafing: it had disappeared by the time the Christmas lunch was brought to the table and I had dived head first into the 'Scotland Box' in which the wondrous tartan tin of Edinburgh Rock – better than the bows on the Beetons' tree – was buried. Thick sugar sticks in lilac, apricot and green, vanilla white and strawberry pink. Nick and I 'baggsed' the colours that we wanted, squabbling over the pink.

Hopie carved the meat and dispensed the roast potatoes and the gravy, the cauliflower cheese and baby peas.

'The bloody turkey's raw again,' Jumbie said, exasperated.

'Let's call it our tradition,' said Hopie lightly, spooning hot sage and onion stuffing onto his plate.

'I really don't know why we keep him on. He was drunk as a monkey and stinking of *skokiaan*,' Jumbie said, warming to the subject.

'Here!' Hopie pounced on one of the cheap crinkle-paper crackers by her plate. 'Who's going to pull this with me?'

I was afraid of the snap and the smell of gunpowder.

Nicky was not.

I said instead, 'Father Christmas was going to bring Bessie a doll that wets itself.'

'God Almighty,' Jumbie muttered. 'What next?'

– Not in front of the children, dear: I waited for it but it went unspoken: Ninngy was saying grace to herself – as she always did – long inured to our spiritual carelessness.

And so the shadow-side of Christmas has haunted me, vague and unresolved as the strange gaunt reflection of the Christmas tree with thorns, whose streamers lightly ruffled up across the whitewashed wall, a presence which retreated when the multicoloured lights came on and every bauble twinkled back its spark of fire. Some faint anxiety and fear was shrugged off too, back into the cardboard box when we took the decorations down, dismantling the limestone crib. Then the holidays entered the phase of happy aimlessness, 'bush days' in my tree or mornings with Hopie. She piled as many children as she could into the Morris Minor and trundled over the grids and along the road to the beach.

We ran wild along the sucking lines of surf, picnicking beside the Pool-with-the-Rock-in-the-Middle where the smallest children played in safety and the bigger made their pirate ships and castles among the piled rocks around its edge.

Here were waves that fizzed among the gullies and fishing rods made of sticks and nylon. We hunted guppies in the pools and gathered when we were hungry to split open a watermelon with a knife. It was ice-pink and cold with lines of slippery black seeds which we spat in competition with each other, arguing the distance, making boats from the rind. And coming home, sunburned, a wisp of salty hair sucked at the corner of a mouth, sand caught in little pockets in elasticised costumes, the smell of sun-warmed rubber from a bathing cap, Hopie would slow at the bee-eaters bank. She would motion us to silence, straining for the sound.

I can still hear their call, see the swift flash of wings: the green and blue and gold.

Our Christmas birds.

I wonder if they nest there still – now that the road has been expanded, tarred and is an artery to town. I suspect they have migrated elsewhere – like the Ragas and the Djantjes. Back to the mysterious, unknown, unrecorded places from which they came.

## CHAPTER ELEVEN
### *Crows*

*T*here were always crows on the playing fields at school. They were there to clean up the schoolyard. The night-shift workers.

We did not have them in the valley – perhaps it was too bushy and dense for crows. They haunted the fields which were brown, drought-blistered stretches cut out between the corridors of brush.

Crows and yucca plants and dust-dry pines.

I remember those yuccas with their fleshy and ambiguous flowers at the edges of the hockey pitch and the crows walking in the morning, hunched in rows.

They scavenged birds' nests too. I know that they took their toll on dikkops and kiewietjies. I had seen the frantic parents playing decoy to a crow and he, capering and gluttonous. They nested near the graveyard on the wind-swept hilltop behind the school where stone pines bowed before the ceaseless blast.

It was a private cemetery, belonging to the convent. The graves of nuns went back a hundred years. Once, Sister Philomena took us there – a raggle-taggle troop of squabbling girls left under her supervision as we waited for the late afternoon lift to come. Perhaps she wanted to place flowers on a recent plot and, unable to leave us unattended, took a chance including us.

She coaxed and cajoled us up the hill and the more compliant helped her gather pink oxalis and put them in the jam jar of water which she carried. We pulled periwinkles with their coin-like leaves and star-blue faces. It was a long path up the hill, mossy in places, the green mounds cushioning rocks beside the track. There was the sound of the wind in the pines and the unexpected clashes in the topmost branches high above. We started at the sudden thuds of falling pine cones, the little after-shock of silence. We paused – alert – then trudged along, our leather-soled shoes slipping on the long, fallen needles of the pines.

The path came to a service road at the top of the hill which led to a water tank and reservoir, barricaded by barbed wire. We were not allowed to go near it. Some menace haunted it: the nuns had a way of spreading innuendo. It made us wary of whatever lurked in the bushes, behind the water tank, at the end of the long school drive. Under the bed.

It was male and hostile.

I could never understand it. Especially as all the males in my life were benign: Jumbie, Gramps, Tom Moreland. What was sinister about men?

Ah . . . Not just men.

Black men.

Sister Evangelist told us – briskly – to check under the bed before getting into it at night: 'Just in case' . . .

It was preposterous! What would Alfred Banda be doing under my bed? Or daft old Tawns with his lop-sided grin? Or aristocratic, dignified Daniel Moreland?

–Do you think the nuns are always right?

–The Pope's infallible, said Hopie enigmatically.


In the graveyard there was a great black-painted wooden crucifix with Christ, bleached white. He looked down on the ranks of iron crosses in their palisaded plots. Here and there a vase was overturned, a dried wreath of flowers rustled faintly. Such strange names: Sisters Servatius and Virgilius and Gonzalez and Mother de Padua.

I always wondered if nuns had ever had real names. If they remembered their birthdays. If they had ever played and shouted and run. If they had longed for Christmas presents.

If they had hair?

If they'd ever kissed a boy.

And what about children? Why would they give up children?

Did they hate them?

Was that why Sister Ignatius used a cane on the upturned palm of even the smallest girls, lined up, hands out, frog-throats alive with fright and eyes hot with shame?

All of them seemed old: they all had milk-pale, blue-veined skin. They were like Nora Moreland's doll with its waxen face. Perhaps, hidden under their cream serge habits were calico bodies, quite detached from flesh, with a hairless head and moulded hands.

Row on row of iron crosses, rusted now by the wind and sun, lay below the looming shadow of the cross, like supplicants. Name on name – and they, as alone in death in the small earth cell as they had been in the whitewashed convent sleeping-cell in life.

'What about their families?'

'God bless you child,' Sister Philomena said. 'We put earthly things away when we take our vows. We are the Brides of Christ.'

'How can He marry all of you?'

'What questions you ask!'

'How can all the nuns be married to Jesus?' This at supper.

'God Almighty.' Jumbie's standard as he dissected the corned beef.

—Not in front of the children.

'It's not exactly marriage,' was Hopie's careful reply.

'What is it then?'

'Communion.'

'That's to do with wine and wafers,' said Nicky.

'Not wine, women and song.' Jumbie again.

'*Really*, dear.' Ninngy put her knife and fork down with a small rattle.

Nicky started to laugh, complicit in the joke.

'I hate corn beef,' I said instead.

'You are the fussiest eater I've ever known.'

–Think of the 'poor children'...

–If you'd been in England in the War...

–There isn't a War...

–I said, 'If'...

So the Bride of Christ remained a mystery until I decided one day that I had a vocation. This, after a visit to the Catholic shop with Steffi Brody, where they sold holy pictures, luminous rosaries, blue-robed Virgin Marys in painted plaster of Paris, the Sacred Heart circled by thorns and Jesus, His head inclined and two fingers raised.

'Why does He do that? Dad does that if another car gets in the way.'

'Does what?' said Steff.

'Shoves two fingers up and yells "Out of the way, fool".'

'He's giving a blessing.'

'Who, Dad?'

'Jesus, silly.'

Such are the inconsistencies.

I said no more about vocations until I saw *The Nun's Story* at the Drive-In when I was supposed to be asleep on the back seat with Nicky after a hot dog and chips from the Silver Slipper Road House.

And that decided me irrevocably.

Such sublime prayers, such poignant beauty, such courage in her fight against 'Archangel Gabriel', the mad woman in her cell.

The Bride of Christ.

Except, I failed to recognise that it was the handsome, brooding mission doctor who lay at the heart of my fascination.

I remember only one funeral in the cemetery at school and the hearse creeping up the sandy track with its flower-laden contents: St Joseph's lilies bobbing their flutes as it passed, small purple tassels fringing a pall, the nuns walking behind – black and white and ponderous, heads down, crow-like. The sound of singing – that low, intoned, ancient chant, novenas for the dead, the translation of another culture, so precisely Eurocentric, onto this thorny hillside where the mimosas drooped pale pollen balls across the sandy banks and puff adders passed undisturbed through thickets.

It was not a funeral for a nun.

It was for a child of three: the baby brother of a classmate.

Perhaps it was the closeness of a staunch Catholic family to the Order, the parents active on the Board, the daughters distributed throughout the school in varying degrees of blonde athleticism that made the extraordinary choice of resting place so apt and comforting to them. Consecrated Catholic ground, safe from fear.

Every child in the school lined the track to the cemetery as the cortège passed, preceded by the Bishop in his purple stole, the massive crucifix of his rosary thumping at the heavy folds of his cloak. A great bird, beaky-nosed.

We stood, rank on rank, perplexed at grief.

And something wrung my heart: one small, fragile, tow-haired boy among the black-clad nuns? On this desolate, loveless hill with the crows? These jagged silhouettes tossed in a wind-white afternoon, piloting the gaunt procession moving up the hill? These black-soled wing-beats?

'God has chosen him to be a special angel.' Sister Philomena's gentle lilting voice.

Why then this delirium of cawing at the keening grief of prayers?

# CHAPTER TWELVE
## *Shrikes*

*T*hat ringing call. Old bokmakierie shouting about the spot where he will make a cattle byre: glad, glorious morning, spring days, plumbago-blue sky and the smell of dust settled by a swift, early-morning rain.

Lesley-Jean and I take the horses down the grass tracks, through the bush, looping and twisting to the goat farm where we stop at the old water trough to let the horses breathe.

Les rides well.

I do not.

She can jump a three-barred fence or a combination, do dressage and go bare-backed.

I am afraid of horses even if I never dare admit it. But they know it – and are tolerant. Especially Rosie.

She is an old, fly-bitten grey with a bow-back: sturdy and complacent – but the wiliest horse in The Bush when she doesn't want to be ridden. She can bolt from corner to corner of the paddock, dodging on a whim – far faster and more deft than a much younger animal. But when she is cornered, she seems faintly amused – a wry lifting of her soft lip for the bit. She would give a great sigh, knowing that she and Les's fat mare are off on another predictable meander.

But if she is lazy at the start, she becomes companionable and interested once we've left the road. We walk in single file, vigilant for cars – but when we turn off down on to the grassy pathways almost mown between the ramparts of the coastal bush, we draw abreast and urge them on – a trot, a canter. It is then that a shrike always seems to call, the starting bell to a race, the wild, joyful shout of a summer morning. And we, laughing (me just a touch breathless from fright), duck thorn branches and lift our legs from the catch and pull of the Kei apple bushes growing in disturbed places.

Here is the bou bou's fat contralto, one to the other. Perhaps a glimpse of soft rufous under-flanks, the ash-black wings and hooded head.

We rarely saw them but we heard them and they, of all the birds I know, have their belonging in the thick, black-green undergrowth of milkwood and *isipingo* bushes. They haunt the *boerboon* thickets where the bark puts out waxy red flowers and the blue-green shade of feathered leaves sifts across the undergrowth. And if we never see them, we know they are skulking there, just as we know that the bokmakierie lurks about the edges of the open pasture. Sometimes we see the dash of yellow as he launches from a fence post, shouting:

–Here is my cattle kraal.

–Here the calves increase.

–Here is my packstone wall and aloe hedge; my goats and cows and sheep.

For us it is the clarion call to exploration – and, once again, Les and I explore.

I don't know when it changed, when unease took a grip of me, anxiety at footfalls in the bush, recoiling from a stranger on the path, a certain furtiveness as though there was a watcher.

A loss of trust – when trust was not betrayed.

But it happened unobtrusively – and we stopped our rides, unconstrained by time, or by direction. It seems that those paths and byways – that maze within the corridor of coastal bush – receded, closed over, became unfamiliar. Now, I would not be able to find my way. Then, I could have drawn a map of tree and bush and flower: turn left at the third *boerboon*, keep straight past the dead sweet thorn with the silver bark, go up the dune path where the knobthorns grow. Keep on until you reach the first of the Port Jackson's willows and you can see the sea.

You will find your way. You will hear the shrikes calling.

It was the alien Port Jacksons which caused the destruction of that world. Their relentless thrust into the thick indigenous bush, their ability to burn and explode.

It was Nicky who sensed the fire first.

Nicky, who never rode or came into the bush: some reticence which I did not understand.

Even as a little girl, she would be watching.

And how could I apprehend her fear? I had not seen a family home implode in gusts of flame as she had, even if she had been less than three years old.

She told me – later – how she'd fill up buckets and basins with water whenever the *bergwind* blew. Ever watchful.

We were at school that Saturday, at the gala, the red, yellow and blue of the Houses' bunting lifting in a sudden, unexpected gust. It was a *bergwind* – that dry, lung-filling heat that so enchanted me – and made Nicky instantly alert, a small creature sensing danger long before it has appeared.

Some rumour in the wind. Some scent.

There was a plume of smoke away to the west, so slim, so faint, the passing breeze might have brushed it aside.

But it grew.

No wider, no brisker – but darker.

Nicky left the ranks of swimmers and went to Hopie sitting in the stand surrounded by mothers and fathers – Basil Brody with his ubiquitous Polaroid, Sister Columbanus, taking down the race times at a desk under an umbrella and wearing a pair of sunglasses which looked peculiarly secular and jaunty.

The word went along the rows. Bush families – first Hopie and Jumbie, then Basil, then Les's father, Colin, walking quickly to a better vantage point.

A word with Sister Columbanus and the men left, going as a group.

By the time the mothers reached the turning to our valley with the swimmers, the gala over, fire was raging all along the line of bush that edged the coastal plain, sweeping eastwards.

My thoughts were for the tortoises and buck, the snakes and birds. The eggs and nestlings. But Nicky knew differently. Her understanding held no sentiment: it was pared to survival. More real, more acute, more precise than I could ever know.

We got home through a pall of smoke, ash flying.

Like every other family we watched the approaching turmoil across the thick mass of the indigenous bush, hearing the distant crackle and fizz of Port Jackson leaves exploding, ready with every labourer we could muster. All over The Bush hoses were dragged to garden taps to wet the thatched roofs of houses. At the Edwards' home a chain of men with empty paraffin tins were heaving water from the old swimming pool. The Beetons in their vast swathe of lawn, their iron-roofed house, were safe from flame but hard-pressed to calm the horses. Down in their enclave in the dip, the Brodys had packed the Peugeot with cameras, rare books, antique jewellery and photographs.

–'What about the cats?' I cried, distracting the grown-ups and annoying Jumbie past his patience. –'What about Tawns's donkey?'

Nicky was waiting at the garage door, desperate to have Hopie drive us away. But Hopie was busy with the beaters, armed with a wet sack, her hair tied up in a damp cotton scarf.

Ninngy, ever-vigilant, had Nicky in the crook of her arm, comforting her. The dogs were already in the car with the windows down.

Nothing stirred in the garden. Even the house seemed to crouch among the flower beds.

Would the noise of fire never cease its relentless crackle against the uncanny silence of the waiting bush?

Would the fire engines never come?

The rain came instead.

The wind changed: that sudden shift from inland heat to salt-mist off the sea.

It poured. And poured. Straight, direct and drenching.

A great thudding sheet washing through the grey of smoke and falling ash and out of which emerged the stark black architecture of the trees.

God's intervention: the nuns had been praying on the hill. Even Jumbie kept his peace and said, 'Thank the Lord.'

Hopie was treating minor burns in the kitchen and pouring out mugs of orange squash for helpers.

Nicky, returning to the house, the dogs following, tails down, was sitting in the bath, the cold tap running.

I wish I'd known her terror and stopped wailing on about the Brodys' cats.

She never wailed. She stared at the taps, her arms tight across her chest.


Despite the rain, in the more sheltered places across the dunes where the Port Jacksons had been thickest, there was still warm ash days later, brittle as burned hair. The whole aspect of the dunes had changed. Where there had been groves and thickets, now there was blackened sand and iron skeletons of brush, singed leaves hanging, the spiral pods of seeds, black cinders scattered on the ground.

We found the burned shells of tortoises: young and old, large and very small, the charred remains of a snake, a buck already doomed by a wire-noosed trap.

The landscape was completely desolate.

No bird called. No clarion shrikes enticing us to follow.

And childhood, somehow, slipped away.


Is it sound, is it scent or is it taste that is the instant conjuror of memory?

It seemed so many years before I heard a bou bou shrike again. Walking on a beach, weary with loss, tracing the nap of salty wavelets breaking where the sea snails made their tracks in thin-frilled circles in the wet sand, watching white-fronted plovers skitter, blown ahead like little balls of spume, I heard a shrike calling from the trees beyond the dunes: that littoral edge where beach meets bush.

Such a lifting of the heart – instant – ringing glad.

Childhood flooded back: its happy ambiguities, its fragile losses, its immortal hopes.

I ran, leaping my reflection where the waves sucked back, scattering the plovers into flight, shouting to the shrike, the shrike shouting back.

As I turned home at dusk, the moon rose full across the sea, not high and white and cold but warm and golden pale: a moment of reprieve before the dark.

Despite its heart of ice.

## CHAPTER THIRTEEN
## *Doves*

*T*he Red-Eyed Turtle Dove: fat and drowsy and domestic. Farmyards, orchards, the sun just going off the boil in the vegetable garden, still too hot to water.

But not too hot to pick peas or dig up carrots and tiny turnips.

Nicky and I wash them under the tap by the coal shed where the home-made ladder with its crooked struts makes a crazy shadow up against the whitewashed wall. The ginger cat, Boy, Brownie the dachsie, various scraggy bush fowls pecking in from James Raga's side of the fence – all come to see what we are doing.

Doves cooing peacefully mean that there is nothing menacing about the bush this afternoon: no snakes in the garden, no meerkats watching from the brush. We sit in the shade and eat the carrots, more metallic than sweet; the turnips, crisp and pungent; shelling the little green peas into our laps, popping them against the roofs of our mouths.

Between the rows of beans and beetroot laughing doves forage. No plumage is as gentle: pewter-grey and rose and blue. *Nokhuthuka*, the little frayed one, boasting that she comes from Xhosaland.

No one seems to notice them. Yet, what would the garden be without them? Like the call of the red-eyed turtle dove, they are security and comfort.

Sometimes we find a dead dove. Then we have a funeral. We will ferret a shoebox out of Hopie's cupboard, tossing her evening sandals aside and smoothing the tissue paper to wrap around the body. The weight and warmth, the lolling head with the strange naked skin that closes the eyes, the colour of the feathers on the breast, a blush across the sombre mauve and grey. We place the corpse in the box and tie it up with a piece of string.

We dig a hole but the soil is dry and hard and we get bored before it is deep enough so that a corner of the box is sticking out. That is not important – making the cross out of straight bits of tomato box and writing '*Dove*' and the date, '*1957*', is the interesting part. And weaving a wreath from canary creeper and sticking pansies or daisies into it and standing mournfully around, heads bowed.

Nicky reads the best so she is the priest with the prayer book. I am better at weeping, so I weep! If Bessie is with us she is earnest and plump, rattling the rosary and closing her eyes very tight. None of us are Catholics but we know the Catholic prayers because of school.

*Oh most gracious Virgin Mary . . .*

'What's a virgin?' Bessie says suddenly snapping open her eyes.

'It's not "a virgin", it's "Virginmary" – that's her name.'

'No, it's not!' Bessie is indignant. 'She's Mary! Same as in Jesus and Joseph and Mary. I was Mary in the play. Don't you *know*.'

'It's not the same person!'

'Yes, it is!'

The funeral stalls, the dove forgotten.

Nicky takes a swipe at us and tells us to get on with the prayers.

If the Brodys are there then Steffi is the priest instead. She has been to lots of funerals so she knows how it's done. Being a Catholic, she is in the choir at church and they often sing when someone dies. They have tea and cake afterwards in the Church Hall. Hopie calls it macabre. She does not approve of children going to funerals.

On any pretext.

It is not good form.

On other days, when the Brodys troop up from their house a mile down the road and Bessie is delivered in the big black car, we will play Pirates on the garage roof until the doves stop cooing and the bulbuls start to chatter up their evening chorus and the drongo – last to bed – chivvies from the vantage of the telephone wire.

Then, after Oros and Marie biscuits, Hopie will invent a game which, I know, has an ulterior motive. Nicky and I exchange a knowing glance as she froths up blue washing powder in the big, sloping double wash tubs in the backyard, bringing a kettleful of hot water to take the chill off the top and scrubs the lot of us in batches. The most enthusiastic in the game is Bessie who loves to slither about in the suds, a marvel of glee despite being the only one among us who does not need a wash. Her glossy little head of straight brown hair is always neatly cut and combed and fastened sideways with a clip.

It is the Brodys who are Hopie's object. They are always in want of a wash and Hopie sets-to with a bar of Sunlight soap, sudsing their tow-coloured hair (five grubby heads, five grubby necks) and scratching the soap into their little scalps with gentle nails.

Their own bathroom with its vast plate glass window and a fine view of the bush-fringed lawn – whether in the bath or enthroned on the loo and public to the scrutiny of all passersby – is a playroom rather than a place of business. No one cares who washes: just as long as they have fun.

And they do.

Mostly squirting the telephone shower at each other 'til the floor is awash and the towels lie sodden on the old linoleum.

They go home from Penderley as neat and brushed and gussied-up in our spare pyjamas as Bessie in her still-pristine frock. Hopie delivers them in her Morris Minor and someone begs that we should be allowed to stay the night.

Sometimes we can. Sometimes we can't. Sleepovers are all the rage.

Except – always – in the middle of the night, if the eagle owl calls or the dark throbs with silence, I wish that I could run down our familiar passage past the bathroom door, setting the small flame of the paraffin night-lamp to waver as I pass, and burrow into Hopie's bed.

I swear I'll never ask to sleep away again.

But I always do: it's fine to swagger when the sun is high and the doves are cooing in the trees.

Doesn't Hopie *know* she should say 'No' when I ask or someone (Bessie hopping from leg to leg) begs to let me stay?

Hopie has forgotten.

Or thinks I've changed my mind.

Doesn't she *know* that something might happen to her in the night?

When I go home she might be gone.

What would she do without me? Tell me *that*!

But when I do go home she is always there and that little fear coiled in my heart – that small, grey doubt waiting to be proven right – is banished with a leap into her arms. Nothing has happened. Everyone is here. There are no Jackie Hangers skizzing warnings from the hedge, no owls glaring their malevolence.

Here is Boy, the ginger tom. And Brownie, the sausage dog. And Ninngy – as peaceful as if nothing untoward had ever happened. Here is Nicky making toffee in the kitchen and smudging sugar all over the stove. Here is Jane singing in the yard:

*The cheap chocolate girl,*

*My mother used to tell me –*

*Tell me a stowery,*

*A story of Loooove,*

*About the cheeeeep choc-o-late girl.*

I sing it too – even if I don't know what it is all about. It is catchy, it synchronises with the plop of the mop in the bucket. It is bluesy and mellow.

Ninngy is having tea on the veranda, sitting always with her ankles crossed, Brownie lying at her feet. I curl up beside her. The plump cooing of the doves in the garden drifts in and Hopie, dashing out to gather up a cup, trails her hand gently across my head as she passes.

'What happened to my shoebox?'

No need to say. I stretch and yawn and close my eyes.

I feel enfolded by a wing.

**CHAPTER FOURTEEN**
# *Game Birds*

*T*here were no game birds at Penderley that I can remember. No guineafowl or francolin. And yet there must have been for that coastal bush was interspersed with open grassland which seemed ideal for nesting, feeding, hiding. Perhaps they had been poached-out, dog-hunted, man-hunted, snared. The first I knew of them was from the pictures in the Beetons' dining room. But, of course, those were English birds: grouse and partridge and pheasant. Stately and restrained among the bracken, set in double, gold-edged mounts. A series, hung together.

I loved their colouring – the browns and buffs and rusts. I used to stand on tiptoe and look at them, wanting to touch the speckled feathers with a finger. On another wall were hunting prints: red-jacketed riders on horses with arched necks and starting eyes and mottled hounds that seemed ready to dash from their frames. On the sideboard nearby was a big porcelain water jug with a hunting scene on it as well. I was mesmerised. When it was picked up it played a tune:

*D'ye ken John Peel*
*With his coat so gay…*

In the nursery was an antique grey dappled rocking horse with a real horse-hair mane and tail that creaked on its stand when we rode it and had just such an arched neck and flaring nostrils as the horses in the prints. Ben and Doss, Bessie's brothers, would ride it so furiously its stand would propel it, thumping across the wooden floor until Nursie came and told them to stop.

But most beautiful of all were the old silver cock and hen pheasant on the dining room table in the shadow of the silver rose bowl. He stood, head turned, one leg raised, alert and regal, his tail making its own sliver of shadow on the polished wood while his plump hen foraged at his foot.

They had a story. Doss and I made it up together, sitting cross-legged under the table. They lived in the grounds of a castle; they were never shot and stuffed and eaten; they prowled the dining room at night, wings lifted as they flushed down to the floor to tread a stately minuet across the Persian rug. In the morning they were back in their place, just as poised as the day before.

Doss knew, I knew: they breathed under their shining feathered armour.

We did not have such a pair of pheasants on our table at home. It was scratched despite the weekly rub of Cobra polish and the best we seemed to do for a centrepiece was a flat, green bowl stuffed with rusty chicken wire to support a bunch of bristly zinnias. No roses here. No pink camellias or heady gardenias with their white waxy flowers to scent the rooms.

Perhaps it was the glamour of the pictures of the game birds, the pheasant and his hen picking their way on their silver toes across the polished table, which made me believe – mist and bracken, tweed and whisky, handsome Bill Beeton in his jodhpurs and his dubbined boots – that a bird hunt would be romantic, an echo from the stories that Doss and I made up when Ben and Bess had gone to boarding school and he was left alone at home.

But it wasn't. It was bloody and vile.

Despite the camaraderie – the suave, predatory male mystery of it all.

It was a guineafowl hunt in winter.

A farm nestled among low green hills with copses of gum and oak and willow. The indigenous bush had been pushed back to river ravines, the grassland ploughed for crops.

It was an old farm and the annual hunting season went back years in the memories of farmers and of workers – a festive time when the flocks of guineafowl were decimated for another year. Neighbours came, trucks arrived, jolting along the red rough road, men in deerstalkers, boys in jeans and fleece-lined jackets, women flocking too, into the living room for tea. Awkward girls with nowhere to go sulked in the winter sun, not included.

Outside the black farm children waited to act as beaters. A ragged motley crowd of thin-shanked boys in discarded jackets, balaclavas, ash-black skin and snotty noses wiped on the back of a sleeve, bare feet or boots or shoes without the laces. They laughed together. Shy, aloof, excited or detached – there was every permutation.

They were sent away at a word into the lands, spreading out to turn and beat the birds towards the waiting guns. They advanced rhythmically, hour after hour, through pasture, donga, camp or mealie field.

I – straying – joined their lingering line and felt the shot patter in the dried-out maize stalks all around me. Little beads of iron rain.

A startled eye, a child ducking, another laughing and, far off, the crack of the rifles, the puffs of smoke, the silence, the sudden flurried burst as birds took flight. Wing beats, an airy somersault, the crash into the undergrowth. Boys running – and still the pattering shot.

All in a day's sport, did it matter that there was a small child detached from his companions, startled by the barrage, lost, frightened, not sure which way to go? No head-count taken, the bakkies bumped away with their cargo, barely stopping to check that the children racing after them had time, from opening a gate, to clamber up again. Spinning wheels, shouts and laughter, the fright of a missed footing, a child left forlorn beside a gate to walk home disconsolately through the cold wind.

Someone saw a hare, pointed as it jinked and dodged from the passing wheels. One of the young men, all bravado, grabbed a shotgun. A foot on the running board, he aimed and fired. The thin thud of bullet striking bone.

'Got him in the eye!' Triumphant.

The hare is tossed onto the back of the truck. A momentary prize. One eye closed quite meekly, as if in acquiescence. The other gone.

The birds are laid out in the pantry behind the fly screen. The blood is congealing here and there on the cool concrete floor. Thirty-seven birds.

—What will happen to them all?

Do the beaters get a bird? After all, they are waiting at the kitchen door. It is cold now and the sun is starting to wane and sink below the hills. The bitter chill and damp will come up through the ground, numbing the bones. Tea trays laden with banana bread and scones are trolleyed through to the living room. The languid girls become animated, the boys shrug off their fleece-lined jackets and sling them on the backs of chairs, someone's wife is sitting on the sofa by the fire knitting booties in blue wool, the decanters are drawn. Brandy, whisky, beers for the boys. The wives call for gin and tonic.

Dusk is swift, the sky a livid yellow way behind the gaunt poplars. There is still a huddle of small boys beside the back door, sunk in against each other, seeking warmth. I do not know what they are waiting for: the guineafowl are all apportioned out.

And they have been forgotten.

In the back of the truck, the tip of each hair frosted now with ice, the hare lies blind, forgotten too.


The hunts Doss and I invented were quite different – and, to my knowledge, he never hunted with a gun. There was no quarry – only a vague sense of a tradition; no dead fox, only the liver-spotted hounds, haloo-ing. No kill – only the jolly hunting horn and stout John-Peel-in-his-coat-so-gay.

Doss had a little green-brown hacking jacket with leather patches on the elbows, an echo of his father's. In it – with his tanned, freckled face, his turned-up nose, his pudding bowl of brown hair streaked with lights – he was as mottled as a partridge: speckled warm. I might find him in the paddock, lost among the deep swells of thick Kikuyu grass, his crop in his hand, his riding hat too big for him, the tips of his pink ears poking out, waiting for the groom to bring his pony. He rode with a straight back, never failed to keep his toes up, brushed down his horse, saw to her hooves, fed her oats. She followed him as if she were his shadow, nuzzling at his neck.

He did not often venture out on her alone. Instead, he rode her in the paddock – precise, schooled, neat and at one. Determined on correctness.

It was something he did well: to ride like a gentleman, to jump with considerate hands, to keep his seat like a true horseman. The rosettes on his bedroom wall were testimony to his skill.

But he did not go to school.

He was kept back. Too delicate, too anxious, too dyslexic to be educated. That's what was said.

Of course, it wasn't all the truth.

He had the most enquiring and perceptive mind. Nothing passed his notice, his interest or his quaint, wry scrutiny; his touch of humour, his candid innocence.

They made an invalid of him.

Lovingly. Unthinkingly.

It was a time when no one knew much better – long before the 'experts' flooded the market or 'psychology' became respectable.

A private tutor was employed. And in the afternoons I sometimes went to play.

Then we made our own inventions, our empires and our kingdoms. Our intricate histories, our gallant heroisms: Doss in his hacking jacket and his boots, expansive in his fantastical world, listening for the flush of the pheasant's wing, the secret cipher to all our games.


I grew up first and went away.

I forgot about the pheasants. And Doss – suspended – was put aside like the dusty treasures I had placed so carefully on my window ledge.

Oh Doss – when, in all the years that followed, did your endearing quaintness turn to oddity, your individuality transmute to haunting loneliness?

And what of us who knew you – and our trite and careless condescension?

He inherited the family home and all the accoutrements of childhood: the rocking horse, the hunting prints, the jug, the game birds and the partridges – they with their silver-armoured wings, their midnight minuet.

He died there too.

Alone and weary.

It was not a cry for help. It was decisive and courageous.

Daring the silence.

That quaint, unswerving honour, that ardent soul.

I hope the pheasants bore that soul away to where the gallants fight with tempered steel, where there is nothing bloody or vile.

Where the hare scents the dawn, alert and unafraid.

And the pheasant steps, high-toed, beside his hen.

## CHAPTER FIFTEEN
## *Jiza Birds*

*W*ho knows the *jiza* bird? They are those small prinias, warblers and cisticolas which are rarely seen, fret-feathered filaments of down, bright-eyed and nameless, dusky denizens of the secret bush. They have their hidden wisdom and society, known by their small throaty murmurings – warning of a presence, a swift alert at a quiet footfall on a path.

But *jiza* birds are more than that.

In bird-lore they have the wisdom of ages, calling, *mvi, mvi, mvi vityori*.

The warbling little flute; the comforter of birds that dwell by the river. The secret watchers in the shade.

All of our bush was alive with them – but in the places where I could not go for the undergrowth was far too thick, the thorns too dense, the rustlings in the brush too threatening to try. Yet, like the *jiza* birds, itinerant woodcutters such as Tawns and Gracie, lived in the smallest enclaves in the thickets, undiscovered, unremarked, but for a slim thread of smoke among the Port Jackson willows from a cooking fire or the droppings of a donkey somewhere on a black-sanded track. And sometimes, on the road, laden with logs, we would see their felt-brown donkey beaten to a trot, pulling an old cart bearing the harvest away, children perched on top. They would disappear into the township beside the railway line – that squatter-camp, that unknown undergrowth of shacks, ash-heaps, alleyways and plots of arid ground.

They would return when their wood was sold and dissolve again into the bush. Sometimes I would hear the chock-chock-chock of an axe, like a distant bird call, a tinker barbet tapping his tiny anvil. *Jiza* birds, far off in another world: the outliers of the farms where the brush and thickets, limestone slabs and stagnant pools lie forlorn and unclaimed all the way down to the coast.

One evening, just as it was almost dark, there was knocking at the back door.

It was not loud. But there – persistent. Tap-tap-tap. A beak pecking: tap-tap-tap; tap-tap-tap.

Hopie went.

It was Tawns.

His daughter had been bitten by a snake. He did not know what snake because it had happened at dusk when she had been gathering wood. Ten years old and hauling logs.

The bite was big. He held up crooked fingers, an inch apart. '*Pofadder, missis. Seker 'n pofadder.*'

He had carried her on his back, half an hour through the bush and laid her down just outside the perimeter of the yard, a small bundle in a wisp of frock.

Hopie brought a torch. The bite was in the shin, just above the ankle.

We put her in the car. Jumbie drove. Hopie, Nicky and I sat in the front and Tawns in the back with his daughter in his arms.

No one spoke.

I remember the road, the headlights wavering along it, the rhythmic ring of the iron ribbing of the grids, the whoosh and bump as the car hit the other side, the wire fences shredding the passing beams, a heliograph flashing along the edges of the track. The looming gums at the turning to the tarred road.

'Go to the Provincial,' Hopie said. 'It's closest.'

Every now and then I turned to look at Tawns and his daughter, heard Hopie's small clucks and whispers of encouragement. I held her sleeve as if, in clenching the cloth in my fist, I could sustain life.

I said my prayers, silently. Every single one I knew – and started all over again.

I knew that Nicky was doing the same.

We reached the hospital, its lights in serried rows, the great door blazing forth, a white ambulance disgorging a patient. There was relief in hearing our tyres swish reassuringly across the turning circle to the entrance.

Hopie climbed out, hurrying. Suddenly, I felt her calm slip as she disappeared through the door, able – at last – to pass responsibility to someone else.

It seemed that she was gone for hours. At last we saw her silhouette, running now.

She opened the door, ducked in and closed it with a jerk. She said, 'They won't take her. We have to go to Livingstone.'

'God Almighty,' Jumbie, beginning to climb out.

'No,' Hopie said. 'It's useless. I shouted my head off but no one cared. She's black and they won't admit her.'

That night remains a turning point. A signal moment in my life. A knell.

It seemed that no one breathed.

Jumbie did not know the way to go. Hopie was unsure. Tawns's quiet instructions from the back of the car were our only guide.

*'Draai Baas, links Baas. Regs by die straat daaronder. Daaie een. Daar's sy.'*

And then the undertone of Xhosa to his daughter: small sounds, crooning.

Livingstone Hospital, in its vastness, floated like a battleship above the sea of scattered lights: the great edifice of red brick, its windows like a hundred portholes, the gale thudding up against its weight. The parking lot was choked with cars even in this early dark, the flare and dip of headlamps, the movement of people across the bare windows, the long skeins sitting on benches by the walls, waiting, waiting, waiting.

We could not wait.

Hopie was firm now, imperious. And, yes – using her whiteness to gain instant attention.

She did it because she had to. There was no time to lose.

Tawns carried his daughter in. She was put on a stretcher, her leg weeping plasma, the flesh beginning to corrode, insensible now. They were sucked into the fluorescent labyrinth, Hopie going ahead.

Nicky and I sat in the car with Jumbie. He was drumming with his fingers on the wheel, his face set. He lit a cigarette.

'Why wouldn't they take her at the other hospital?' Nicky asked.

'Because she's a native.'

'But she could die.'

'As if they care.'

'Why don't they care?'

'Not now, Ponko,' he said quietly and lit another cigarette. The first was still burning with its small red tip resting in the ashtray.

He had forgotten all about it.

Tawns's daughter did not die. She stayed in hospital a long time. Hopie fetched her back one morning when we were all at school, gaunt old Tawns going with her in his overcoat. I did not see her, not even perched on the top of the cart when we met it on the road. Months and months went by. But, one day, when I had followed a path leading from my tree, deeper into the brush than I had been for weeks, I came across her suddenly.

Like a *jiza* bird, startled in its foraging, constrained – like any bird – to forage where it must, instantly poised to dart away, she turned and looked at me without a hint of recognition in her face.

I glanced involuntarily at her leg. There was a deep depression on her shin, the skin grafted back as if it was burned against her bone.

I raised my hand and greeted her.

'*Molo*,' she replied in an undertone and went on with her task. I stood uncertain until she suddenly withdrew.

There, then gone – like a neddicky, slipping beneath a twig, made invisible by shadow. Just the brush of a leaf, a twitch of light trembling as it passes.

*Mvi, mvi, mvi vityori.*

There was a hush before a small wind tipped the leaves.

Or was it just a *jiza* bird, darting swiftly out of reach?


'Why wouldn't they help Tawns's daughter at the hospital?' I said to Hopie when we sat at supper.

'Because they couldn't,' Hopie said.

'Hah!' Nicky – accusing and triumphant. 'You always say you don't believe in "*couldn't*"!'

'I don't,' said Hopie quietly. 'And I never will.'

# CHAPTER SIXTEEN
## *Wagtails*

There is a mythology of wagtails. Half an ounce of grey feathers and yet so much gravitas! It has always belonged to the herdboys – those who follow the cattle and the calves to pasture. The sanction on hunting it is fierce. Never kill a wagtail for then, the calves will die. Never harm or harry it for the herd will fail to thrive. To betray it is cowardly and cruel. If it should be accidentally killed it should be buried with a small white bead in propitiation:

> *Camagu! Mandingafikelwa ngamashwa.*
>
> *Let misfortune pass me by.*

It is a time-honoured inversion: that the small, innocent and vulnerable should transcend the power of eagles, despite its unobtrusive modesty.

All over our lawn there would be wagtails. Singly and in pairs, sometimes in family parties, sometimes little flocks, hunting midges and small insects, flying off with a quick chirrup of alarm, always vigilant. No more happy an association than a wagtail on the path tiptoeing on the bricks with its delicately balanced tail – that face, that eye, that trusting innocence.

They were companions in the garden with the tortoises that plied across the wide expanse of lawn, wavering slightly as the wagtails wavered, as if heading into a wind, their carapaces grey, charcoal-ridged, the same dove-colouring as the little birds.

Ninngy loved the wagtails and the tortoises too and I have always associated them with her. Dressed in grey with a close creamy cloth hat on her head, slow and deliberate with her can and her trowel, she was as familiar a sight in the garden as they were. Neither ever seemed to shy away from her or be alarmed for she moved gently, trustingly.

When I was small I would go with her, happy to trot about behind her, vigilant as she was to each flower, a baby tortoise with a fragile shell, a wagtail's nest somewhere in the thick tecoma hedge. I can smell still the scent of water on hot, black, sandy soil as she carefully tended the round bed of pansies, all the velvet faces turned up to the sun.

She used to read to Nicky and me: that soft voice with only the hint of a Scots accent, the last vestige of her girlhood. She chose the books, directing us. They came from her own collection, some leather-bound in burgundy or green with gold-tooled letters and water-marked end-papers. And if my heart has always searched for heroes, it was Ninngy who gave them to me first: explorers, mountaineers, buccaneers and soldiers. Kings and knights and cavaliers. King Arthur and his gallant band; Scott and Peary and Hillary. Like Alfred Banda with the hare and tortoise, she, too, retrieved her past with words. And through those words we gained another history and a clear aesthetic.

The acutely observed worlds of those two great storytellers in my life – Alfred Banda and Ninngy – lodge in my heart, not in opposition despite the great difference in tradition, but in the shared nobility of words.

We sat, we listened, we remembered.

For Nicky, poetry became her leitmotif.

For me, imagined landscapes: a pantheon of place.

But sometimes we baulked at the thin-leaved volumes with the splinter of gold along the knife-edge of the page and the crafted crest on the cover: we wanted some trite, fashionable book with comic-strip pictures we'd got from school. And sometimes we were truculent and cruel.

Ninngy was deaf and occasionally, when there was some particularly noisy pop-group playing on the radio – Nicky was devoted, at this time, to the hit-parade – one of us might say, exaggerating: 'Oh, Ninngy, listen! The bagpipes!'

Then she would sit near the radio, rapt – believing – her eyes focused middle distance and down. And, as some band thumped and twanged, she transposed the sounds into the pipes haunting the heather-covered hills of her childhood home.

As we laughed covertly, hiding where she couldn't see us – mocking, cruel – she would stay, head bent, unmoving.

How could we know? We who had never been displaced from home, who had never had to question our belonging or leave each dear association?

I pay for that now.

Deservedly.


–Please don't die tonight.

I had been invited out – a first real date. In the middle of the night, only hours before this great event, Ninngy had a severe palpitation. The family doctor was called – he with his gaunt grey face and his corrugated hair, his loose limbs and loose suit and big black bag. I sat up in bed in the next room with my heart pounding. Not for Ninngy – but in case she should die and I was stopped from going in my bright floral mini and new pinching sandals.

–Please don't die.

She didn't die and I went out – happily and even memorably – and almost as sophisticated as Nicky who (perfect tan, sleek hair, eyes heavy with false lashes and black liner) was already a stranger in the house, collected and delivered in a variety of cars by alarming young men.

I was too shy and awkward to talk to them. Besides, they did not meet my view of heroes: there were no explorers or game rangers or fighter pilots among them, just fellows from Nicky's last year at school or a rep from a sweet company with blazing blue eyes and an unsuitable accent which displeased Jumbie disproportionately.

Even Hopie bridled against her usual generosity.

Nicky was firm.

She did as she wished while Bess and I wrote messages in our diaries as if they were autographs from boys – hoping Bessie's brother Ben would read them and be amazed.

He was not so foolish.

We became – turn and turn about – the brunt of his scorn and handsome patronage.

–Your thighs are fat. This, to his sister.

–*Muntu*-mouth, your lips are huge. Mouthing off at me.

It made no difference to devotion. I loved him deliriously.

But that was childhood being shed, stepping out of the chrysalis.

It was not first love.

Of course, Ninngy no longer read to us. Once, she had ensured we did our homework, cut our sandwiches for school herself, pottered in the kitchen baking baps or scones or peanut biscuits. Now, Nicky and I took to nibbling Provita and Marmite without butter and inspecting our thighs in the mirror. The meringues went soggy in the cake tin unless Jumbie – always considerate to his mother – dutifully ate them.

Nurturing became redundant: we did what we wanted for ourselves. I learned my work alone, no longer including Ninngy in my revision or asking her to test me as I used to do, gleaning – unconsciously – more education from her than I ever got in the classroom.

She withdrew acceptingly.

She spent all day in the garden with the tortoises and wagtails. I would not have known it then, but I know it now – despite her love for us (and even her dependence) she was withdrawing into the reservoir of memory that leads one back to the beginnings – and its sad autonomy.

It is such a solitary thing, to be alive.

It was a Sunday and I was sixteen. Bess and I had been invited to the beach by brothers on their Sunday exeunt from school. We could not go without Hopie promising to drive us.

We begged and begged.

And so we set out on a shining summer's morning.

We had a picnic basket, cold drinks, a cooked chicken, mounds of tuck for the boys to take back with them to school. We dressed ourselves for hours, trying to look unconcerned, squabbling over the best bikinis in Nicky's cupboard while she was away and could not catch us at it.

Sometimes the world is complicit. And this day it was.

Hopie took her painting box and sat on a rock far away from us, absorbed in a watercolour, her little towelling hat on her head, while we wandered in an airy world of rock and sea and sky and dune, the gulls flying ahead with long strokes, planing and landing, strutting and then lifting off as we approached to veer across the sea and circle in behind us.

We peeled off in pairs.

There is a silence in those great dunes: the shadows are blue in the soft, high hollows and in the dips stones have sometimes gathered where sea birds lay their eggs. The higher we climbed towards the seam of bush at the crests, the more distant the surge of the surf, the more pungent the smell of loam and *blombos*.

How well recalled – that salty kiss.

The sky an aching blue and close by on a rock, a small grey wagtail standing fine-toed in its tiny pool of shadow. Attentively, we watch it because we cannot look too closely at each other in that shy and breathless afternoon.

Hopie drove us back to the school, sunburned, salty, surging with happy exultation, all four of us crammed in the back of the car, sweaty fingers interlinked, still not looking at each other, still too tentative to dare.

And yet, there is nothing quite as intimate as holding hands.

Little children know that well.

So do the dying.

We got home in the twilight and unpacked the car. Jumbie and Ninngy had been alone at home all day. They had eaten lunch together in the garden under the flowering *keurboom* and he, unusually, had helped her water seedlings.

She had cooked us supper.

I said goodnight to her by the passage door. She was wearing her little old red frock with the elasticised waist and the white flowers patterned all over it. She took my hand and held it a moment in hers. 'I'm glad you're happy, my darlin',' she said.

It was a benediction.

I found her when I went to say Good Morning before going off to school. She lay on her side and her cheek was resting gently in her palm. Only by the quiet slackness of her face, I knew – and fled.

I was made to go to school, told to say nothing. There was to be no change and even her teacup and her breakfast tray which Hopie had been busy setting in the kitchen were laid out in their usual place as if nothing had happened.

That afternoon – suspended – I stood in the garden. It was just the same: the flowers were in their beds, the pansies with their upturned faces, the sweet alyssum clambering among the limestone edging of the borders.

And I bridled – because I was young and unthinking – against its being the same when she had gone.

Now I know that sameness is the consolation, the core of all remembrance, often lodged in small and unobtrusive things: the thread of music, the bird call, the dusty scent of stocks in the heat of this empty afternoon. These do not change.

I used to wonder why Ninngy took so many pains with the smallest flowers in the garden. Why, against the blaze of wind, the whipping sunlight, the dry, dry sand, she still planted poppies and snapdragons, pansies and petunias.

It was in faith and in remembrance of something she had lost and needed to hold close.

It is rare to find tortoises in the valley now and wagtails are seldom seen since pesticides have decimated them. Once so ubiquitous and so familiar – as Ninngy was: no lawn without her sturdy figure going about in her delight in growing things.

Until the day that she was gone.

If anything had been alert in that summer dawn perhaps it was the wagtail on the path, the tortoise stopping suddenly: ponderous, attuned.

Through them – their presence and simplicity – something is conferred: a tortoise in the veld, taking its purposeful way, neck outstretched, unblinking; a wagtail in my yard – that cheerful *tseep* of recognition, that small, tendril-tail wavering as it steps across the grass, that merry eye.

Somehow tenderness survives.

# CHAPTER SEVENTEEN
## *Nightjars*

*I* cannot remember the first time I heard a nightjar – but I can recall the last time that I heard it in The Bush on a summer's night when the moon was full and the thin thorns of the mimosa in the paddock made a medley of silver shards, pollen balls like frost. Soft air, *bergwind* night, cobalt sky scattered with stars like a field of flowers in the dark. And then that call – beckoning way off in the deeper bush.

There is no bird more beautiful to me than a fiery-necked nightjar. No sound more evocative or haunting. And nothing that reminds me more of home. And yet – belonging is never sure. Home – like faith, like love – is also tenuous. So is the vagabond born, just like the nightjar – despite cleaving to that old configuration in its heart, of place and of belonging. The comfort of its southern stars. The scent of leaf litter where it lays its eggs, the fret of branches where it rests secure.

First love: that essential pilgrimage.

How memorable. And how absurd.

Young girls, quivering with expectation, nestlings needing to be fed: all down and unfledged wings.

No wonder Hopie smiled.

He arrived one day in the company of an uncle. A young man transferred to our town for three months with no friends, no contacts and nowhere to go.

I suspect Hopie almost fell in love with him herself: his Byronic looks, his urbanity, his mysterious detachment. He could quote Wilfred Owen by the ream. He smoked a pipe, he had a cable knit sweater and looked like Shackleton setting out for the Antarctic. He had every nuance of the poet.

I fell in love.

Hopie had always said that love is dissipated if it's talked about. Like a precious place – it is not something to be lightly shared.

She had her reasons – and she gave me mine.

There remains remembrance of limpid days – fragments of discovery and strangeness. And happy blindness.

It was my last year at school.

Nicky had almost gone away – into the adult world of work and study and responsibility. She drove a car. She had a salary and bank account. She had a steady boyfriend. The explorations of this life of hers she did not share with me.

Why should she? I was just a kid.

But I took my own new experience to school and tended it in secret like a tabernacle's flame.

What a pain I must have been, almost nun-like in my secrecy!

The gods' revenge for self-congratulation: I got a 'chorb'.

It was the most embarrassing pimple anyone has ever had. Like a beacon on my forehead. Like a baby unicorn sprouting a horn. It glowed. It was hard. It throbbed.

It would not go away.

And on the first night of the holidays I was being taken out to dinner.

This was a grown-up thing, a rite of passage.

This was a carnation in a porcelain vase on a white damask table cloth with wine glasses and a menu. This was a blues band on the little stage in front of golden swags of curtain. This was dancing cheek to cheek.

This was not boys at school with tuck in a tin and holding hands in the back seat of the car with your mother driving.

I knew it hadn't happened to anyone in my class. They were all still sitting in the playground eating sarmies and talking about parties with boys at the school next door.

Always the least sophisticated – now I was as mysterious (and as lofty) as a duchess.

Hopie took me to the doctor because I made such a fuss about the chorb. It was the same old family doctor who had attended us all our lives and who had come to Ninngy with her palpitations. Everything about his rooms was monochrome: the eyesight chart on the back of the door, the drooping cream curtain round the couch, his skeletal face, his white coat with the big bone buttons, his black-rimmed spectacles which magnified his eyes enormously. His wild hair. He was the stereotype of a mad professor. I could imagine him swooping bat-like around a lab with hissing Bunsen burners and belljars frothing formalin.

He folded his hands and glanced at Hopie – appreciatively – and back at me in my grey serge pinafore and tie, my long grey socks, my bulky blue blazer.

'What can I do for you, young lady?'

I lifted my fringe and showed him my forehead. The enormous eyes loomed at it, inspecting.

'Ah hah! Acne, I see. Perhaps a sebaceous cyst.'

It sounded so appalling. So repulsive. So completely unromantic.

Hopie clucked. 'Well, just a little outbreak.'

'I have a very special occasion,' I mumbled, prim and hot, 'and I would be glad to be without it.'

'Ahhhh!' He loomed at me again. No doubt he had in mind a debate, an eisteddfod, a school performance. Perhaps – at a push – the matric dance.

Addressing Hopie: 'I can give her a vitamin injection. And she should avoid chocolate.'

'It's tomorrow night,' I said lamely.

He cocked his head enquiringly, his great briar brows flaring up towards his hair.

'There is a rather special young man,' Hopie said, in slight confusion, covering for me but – for once – completely indiscreet.

The doctor blinked. Hopie gave him a charming, half-coquettish smile.

–Don't you remember being young?

The doctor had never been young. Couldn't she see that?

'A little dinner out.'

The doctor looked at her, rather admonishing.

–Is this suitable?

My palms were wet. There were frog-feet marks in my lap where I had pressed them down to stop the sweat.

*Oh most gracious Virgin Mary* . . . (always to be appealed to in an emergency).

'And can I have wine if I've had an injection?' I said with remarkable rashness.

'Certainly not!'


I did have wine. Rather too much of it. My urbane young man ordered me champagne. I drank half a glass with aplomb, afraid to refuse.

We were called from the lounge to the table – duck à l'orange, parisienne potatoes, baby beans and crème caramel. I had to watch the pattern on the carpet at my feet as I walked to my seat: it was fleur-de-lis in rows, stretching down the room.

But for me it was a wild jungle of exotic leaves, tilting provocatively.

He took my arm and smiled.

I wonder how often he gallantly took my arm and smiled – at my naivete, my gaucheness, my quaint enthusiasms, my awful poems, my foolish letters, my needless tears?

In truth, he was a gallant lad: so young, so insecure, despite the pipe and Wilfred Owen.

I think all he wanted was a family – a place to come and have a supper by the fire, a chat to Hopie who – endlessly generous – listened to his stories and mothered him. I think he found it fun to fish with me – an activity I did with bloodthirsty dedication in his company.

Here is my fat pompano, my slimy, mottled rock cod, my silvery cob. I am prouder than a hunter with a record set of horns.

I climbed a mountain with him, walked the beaches, explored the bush, cooked on a fire, made him oats porridge with the quiet piety of a Florence Nightingale when he was sick and Hopie tucked him up in our spare room and gave him aspirin and a hot toddy made with honey and lemon.

Of course he had a girlfriend back at home.

Far older, prettier, more sophisticated, sassier than me. An adult in every way.

He was my fantasy and I his kid-companion. He always treated me that way – but I didn't know the difference then. Hopie had ensured (again, for some unfathomable reason) a dangerous naivete and trust.

Despite the dinner and the wine.


He went away. The day he left had been a Sunday. We went down to the rock pools on the coast with our fishing rods and cast a line or two around the windy gullies. We stayed all afternoon, saying very little.

A moon came up – full and soft across the sea. We sat on the cliff top for a while and watched it.

It was then the nightjar called: *Good Lord Deliver Us.*

That, indeed, was probably his sentiment: delivery from the tears; the face like a frog, swollen with sobs.

But for me, the call of the small, cryptic, monogamous little bird, hidden somewhere in the coastal bush where dusk was drifting in, was the great lament.

Love – and all its loss. An infinity of tears.

I did not lose only him. I lost our home as well.

He drove cheerfully away out of our lives and never came back.

We moved soon after that.

It was too far for Nicky to travel in and out to work. Ninngy had died and her ashes were buried in the deep shade of the top garden where the thrush foraged and the robin came. The property was too big, the house too empty and, at the end of the year, I would be going away to university.

So we sold our home.

Children never have a say in these decisions. There is no reason that they should, but the wrenching out of roots should be a gradual thing. A translocation which is chosen, not imposed.

Within a month the house was sold and Hopie, with her brisk efficiency, was packing up. My childhood relics went the way of all that had gone before: down into the well shaft in the paddock.

Furniture was dispersed. The saddle and the bridle, the horse blanket and the feed bins were given to Lesley-Jean. I watched a train of old, familiar, well-loved objects – the paraffin lamps, the white enamel buckets, the childhood chest of drawers, taken off in a wagon by woodcutters and workers. There was a jumble sale in the yard. Hopie's lovely dresses – the legacy of dances twenty years before – were borne away in plastic bags. I saw a woman walking in the road with a cut off version of her burgundy velvet ball gown.

All the world was overturned – not least by the car which had driven away with the boy in the cable sweater and the heroic pipe. I kept a box in which was a fragment of stone collected on a beach, a lion's tooth that he had given me and – a greatly generous gesture because they had been precious to him – a pair of cufflinks which I have never worn but which I have always loved. Along with an old unsmoked Texan cigarette and a ticket to the Drive-In.

The chorbs subsided as soon as he had gone.

The sweaty hands.

And yet, I sense the greater loss was not the boy.

It was the place.

The night before we left I sat, knees drawn up to my chin, on the window ledge of Ninngy's old room, looking out into the dark across the paddock where the sweet-thorn grew. I heard a nightjar call – far off, way beyond the stables, somewhere in the deeper stretch of land where my milkwood grew, where I had drowsed the afternoons away in my tree among the *jiza* birds.

Gentle, hopeful, beckoning.

I have searched for that nightjar all my life: the configuration of its guiding stars, its sense of clear direction.

And of home.

I am searching still.

## CHAPTER EIGHTEEN
## *Gull*

*A*ll that was long ago. Forty years and more.

But I remain a captive of the birds – the call, the song, the wing-beat which links me place to place.

I have grown up at last, married the man I love (and who I have known ever since he was a boy), had two daughters who have created their own childhood stories and enchantments – their mythologies – and who, in turn, are mothers now. I have sifted the great romance of place and expectation, learned a truth and found my own autonomy, circling, like Ninngy, back to my beginnings.

But one regret remains: that I can't tell Hopie just how much she means to me – even if she guessed (and I suspect she did). Now I know – feeling it myself – how children grow and go and walk away, not in reality, but in the briskness of their lives, their own preoccupations as I did once myself when I was busy with my family, my home, my career, my friends, my life.

My own impatience.

Robin-brisk as she, and mimicking her every move, unwittingly.


Jumbie died and Hopie nursed him to the end devotedly. Just before he died our little daughters danced for him one night and made him laugh. Meticulously, he organised his books, wrote his columns of figures and accounts almost to the last day of his life, made no complaint despite his pain and told the young doctor who had delivered the diagnosis not to fuss – he would see it through.

He did – old soldier that he was.

I was sitting by his bedside when he died. The newspaper was lying on the table, the water glass half-full beside his pillow.

I wish I'd held his hand.

I wish that I'd remembered what that means. Its simple benediction.

Ten years later Hopie married the pilot in the photo in her war-time album. Rex – the man with the face of a king, the ranks of ribbons on his breast, the rows of golden stripes across his cuffs, the Royal Air Force wings resplendent on his chest.

I did not wonder deeply at the time why she chose to go away. I applauded a great romance, the rediscovery of love later in her life, a story which had been suspended for almost fifty years and had come full circle – a novel in itself. A tale to be told.

We all delighted in her happiness.

But on reflection, I wonder, now, if she went because she felt redundant in our lives – if we, her children, had become too busy, too self-absorbed, too stressed by obligation, despite the family occasions, the laughter and the moments shared. Did she feel pushed to the periphery and – generous to a fault, not wishing to intrude – withdraw to forge another life?

I hope she left for love. But if she gloried in her high romance, its destiny, her leading role in a long-forgotten secret story – I fear she may have found that she had changed. Her voice down the telephone, ten thousand miles away, was cheerful, strong and robin-brave.

And yet, I felt the silence in the grace notes as we spoke. The little breaks for breath behind the newsy laughs. The hand I could not touch.

I believe that Hopie, in the quiet refinement of her new and chosen life, was exiled from her real history – and her core.

From us who had failed to apprehend her near mortality.

The sin of our omission.

If Hopie was a robin all her life – in her efficiency and busyness and independence – she had once said to me when we were standing on a beach one windswept afternoon, 'What kind of a bird would you like to be?'

I didn't know. 'And you?' I asked.

'A seagull, flying free! With the wind and the clouds and the wild sea foam!' She had lifted up her slender arms and laughed.

I never forgot that. Even though it slipped from memory for years.

Hopie died in a large English hospital. Rex was with her, devoted – and bewildered – at her side.

So were Nicky and I.

We remembered now to hold her hand.

I remembered, too, that when we were little children Hopie had often sung to us at bedtime before she blew the lamp out in our room.

There was one song that I loved more than all the rest.

She told me later that when she had been in England in the War, seconded to the RAF – young, alone, afraid – she would sing this song quietly to herself, remembering home.

I sang it to her softly: one small voice wavering across the busy morning ward.

She died soon after I was done.

That afternoon when Nicky and I were standing in her room gathering her clothes together, talking, sometimes laughing, sometimes crying, Rex sitting quietly downstairs alone with his thoughts, I glanced out of the window.

Above the dove-cote and the garden shed, the small clipped English lawn and flower beds, the old tiled roofs of houses and the neighbouring trees, a grey gull – vagrant and alone – floated on a thermal, drifting up, up, up into a cloud-white sky.